ISBN 978-0-364-89413-2
PIBN 11282013

This book is a reproduction of an important historical work. Forgotten Books uses
state-of-the-art technology to digitally reconstruct the work, preserving the original format
whilst repairing imperfections present in the aged copy. In rare cases, an imperfection in
the original, such as a blemish or missing page, may be replicated in our edition. We do,
however, repair the vast majority of imperfections successfully; any imperfections that
remain are intentionally left to preserve the state of such historical works.

Dun Building

The Head Office of The Mercantile

Broadway and Rea   treet

New York C

SEVENTY-FIVE YEARS

OF

THE MERCANTILE AGENCY

R. G. DUN & CO.

1841-1916

BY

EDWARD NEVILLE VOSE

Editor, Dun's International Review

PRIVATELY PRINTED

AT THE PRINTING HOUSE OF R. G. DUN & CO.

BUTLER AND NEVINS STREETS, BROOKLYN, N. Y.

MCMXVI

INTRODUCTORY

THE first mercantile agency in the world was established in the City of New York in 1841. The same institution is the first in its field to-day—a record of continuous success and uninterrupted expansion throughout three-quarters of a century. Its growth is a notable example of American perseverance and enterprise. At the start, the concern occupied a single small room, with less than half a dozen clerks, who laboriously copied in longhand a set of reports which filled only a few ledgers. To-day it is an organization having branches in practically all of the principal cities of the United States, and in ninety-six of the strategic trade centers abroad, with upward of ten thousand employees in these offices, and over a hundred thousand representatives in the less important commercial centers, and with many millions of typewritten reports.

While credit is almost as old an institution as capital —banks for the safeguarding of which have existed for centuries—it is a most remarkable fact that it was not in the countries of the Old World, with their highly developed civilization, but in the then raw and sparsely settled United States of America, that the first organization for the protection of credit was perfected. This truly great conception—rivaling many epoch-making inventions in its value to mankind—was given to the world by a New York merchant, and the story of its progressive improvement, year by year, for nearly three generations, is one that has never before been told.

In compiling this brief sketch it was necessary to delve

into numerous dusty archives of the past, to search through files of early newspapers and magazines, and to correspond with nearly two hundred and fifty branch-office managers, present or retired. Few of the builders of The Mercantile Agency realized that they were creating an institution of world-wide interest and importance, and they therefore seldom kept any permanent record of the events with which they were associated. The men who could say of the early history of the Agency, as did Cæsar of the Gallic War, "All of which I saw and part of which I was," have for the most part passed away. Their chief memorial is the great organization to the upbuilding of which they devoted their lives, and which is now everywhere known as R. G. Dun & Co. In this outline history only the leaders in the great host of Agency workers are mentioned individually, but all—like the soldiers in a well-disciplined army—must share the honor of the achievements described.

From the dawn of civilization credit has been recognized as one of the most vital factors of business, without which it would be confined to narrow limits. One of the oldest refer-ences to credit is in the Mosaic laws, where in speaking of the release of debts every seventh year the great lawgiver says: "Every creditor that lendeth ought unto his neighbor shall release it." (Deuteronomy 15:2.) Thus the relation of debtor and creditor was a well-recognized one at that period, 1451 B. C. In one of his orations Demosthenes, the famous Athenian statesman, who died 322 B. C., said: "If you were ignorant of this—that credit is the greatest capital of all toward the acquisition of wealth—you would be utterly ignorant." The American Demosthenes, Daniel Webster, who was in the plenitude of his great powers when The Mer-cantile Agency was established, once delivered the following memorable panegyric of credit:

Commercial credit is the creation of modern times, and belongs, in its highest perfection, only to the most enlightened and best-governed nations. . . . Credit is the vital air of the system of modern commerce. It has done more, a thousand times more, to enrich nations, than all the mines of all the world. It has excited labor, stimulated manufactures, pushed commerce over every sea, and brought every nation, every kingdom, and every small tribe among the races of men to be known to all the rest. It has raised armies, equipped navies, and, triumphing over the gross power of mere numbers, it has established national superiority on the foundation of intelligence, wealth, and well-directed industry.

One of the clearest expositions of the nature and properties of credit ever written will be found in Chapter IX of Book III in John Stuart Mill's "Principles of Political Economy." In this chapter, which treats of Credit as a Substitute for Money, the foremost master in the teaching of this important science says:

Credit has a great, but not, as many seem to suppose, a magical power; it cannot make something out of nothing. . . . Credit being only permission to use the capital of another person, the means of production cannot be increased by it, but only transferred. If the borrower's means of production and of employing labour are increased by the credit given him, the lender's are as much diminished. The same sum cannot be used as capital both by the owner and also by the person to whom it is lent; it cannot supply its entire value in wages, tools and material to two sets of labourers at once. . . . All capital (not his own) of which any person has really the use, is, and must be, so much subtracted from the capital of some one else.

But though credit is never anything more than a transfer of capital from hand to hand, it is generally, and naturally, a transfer to hands more competent to employ the capital efficiently in production. If there were no such thing as credit, or if, from general insecurity and want of confidence, it were scantily practised, many persons who possess more or less of capital, but who from their occupations, or for want of the necessary skill and knowledge, cannot personally superintend its employment, would derive no benefit from it; their funds would either lie idle, or would be, perhaps, wasted and annihilated in unskilful attempts to make them yield a profit. All this capital is now lent at interest, and made available for production. Capital thus circumstanced forms a large portion of the productive resources of any commercial country; and is naturally attracted to those producers or traders who, being in the greatest business, have the means of employing it to most advantage; because such are both the most desirous to obtain it, and able to give the best security. Although, therefore, the productive funds of the country are not increased by credit, they are called into a more complete state of productive activity. . . .

While credit is thus indispensable for rendering the whole capital of the country productive, it is also a means by which the industrial talent of the country is turned to better account for purposes of production. Many a person who has either no capital of his own, or very little, but who has qualifications for business which are known and appreciated by some possessors of capital, is enabled to obtain either advances in money, or more frequently goods on credit, by which his industrial capacities are made instrumental to the increase of the public wealth; and this benefit will be reaped far more largely, whenever, through better laws and better education, the community shall have made such progress in integrity that personal character can be accepted as a sufficient guarantee, not only against dishonestly appropriating, but against dishonestly risking, what belongs to another.

While many writers and speakers have attempted definitions since, no one has ever surpassed this classic passage from Mill with respect to the economic aspects of credit. For our purpose, therefore, it only remains to define credit in its legal aspect, and explain the office of a mercantile agency in relation thereto. This has been very clearly and tersely done by Francis L. Minton, now and for two score years an adviser and director of The Mercantile Agency in its work, as follows:

> Credit, in a legal sense, may be defined as "a right of action." If a merchant enjoys good credit, as it is termed, he may go into the market and buy goods, not with money, but by giving his promise to pay money at a future time for them—that is, he creates a right of action against himself. The goods become his property exactly as if he had paid for them in money. The right of action is the price he pays for them, and the right of action is termed a credit, because it is not a right to any specific sum of money, but only a general right against the person of the merchant to demand a sum of money at a future time. . . . When a merchant purchases goods with his credit instead of with money, his credit is valued in money because the seller of the goods accepts his credit as equal in value to money.
>
> The office of a mercantile agency is to give a merchant information upon which he may determine the value of the right of action which it is proposed he shall accept as the consideration for the transfer of his title to his goods. . . . By far the larger part of mercantile transactions are based upon credit. In other words, by far the larger part of transactions between merchants and manufacturers, which have to do with the passing of the title of goods, are, in effect, a sale of the goods by the seller to the buyer in exchange for the buyer's promise to pay, that is, in exchange for a right of action against the buyer. Credit, then, made up of simple debts, deposits, bills, notes, etc., is the chief medium of exchange in a commercial sense. . . . A well-managed credit amounts to tenfold the funds of a merchant, and he gains as much by his credit as if he had ten times as much money. . . . Credit is, therefore, the greatest wealth to every one who carries on commerce.

According to some authorities the proportion of credit transactions, out of the enormous total to which modern business gives rise, is as large as ninety-five per cent. In fact, it would be practically impossible to carry on the business of the world to-day without credit, and its universal destruction would be an economic disaster of appalling magnitude. In view of the great importance of the subject, it is hoped that this brief history of the first institution in the world for the systematic appraisal and recording of credits will be of interest, not only to the friends and clients of The Mercantile Agency, but to all students of economics and of modern business, and particularly to the great army of credit men upon whose judgment and sagacity the safety of every mercantile community so largely depends.

CHAPTER I

The Inception of The Mercantile Agency

1841–1846

In order to understand clearly how The Mercantile Agency came into existence when and where it did, it is necessary to recall some of the principal characteristics of the American mercantile community of seventy-five years ago. The people of the United States were slowly beginning to realize that they were on the frontier of the greatest and richest wilderness ever thrown open for development. It was a period of feverish mercantile activity during which traders made fortunes in a few years, but with alternate spells of severe and sudden depression when the wealth that had been so quickly acquired was often lost with even greater rapidity.

While pioneers were still blazing trails across the mountains and spreading out along the river systems of the great central plain, the iron horse had come to solve the problem of bringing the products of the interior to the seaboard. Beginning in 1826, a few short lines had been built at various points along the coast until by 1840 the total constructed and in operation was 2,818 miles. By 1852 this had increased to 10,814, and by 1860 to over 35,000 miles. In 1841, however, transcontinental lines were undreamed of, and the great trunk routes to the central plain were just being started. On September 23rd, Philip Hone recorded in his invaluable diary the opening of the Erie Railroad from Piermont to Goshen—not a very long link in the transcontinental chain, truly, but one that had taken six years to finance and build. The inaugural journey was made on platform cars, "exposed to a constant shower of sparks and cinders, like those which accompany a visit to Vesuvius or Ætna, only not half so romantic," the train being "toted by two whizzing, snorting, fire-and-smoke vomiting locomotives." An all-rail journey from New York to either Boston or Buffalo was still a long way off in 1841, although short links had been completed. As late as 1847 the Pennsylvania Railroad extended only from Philadelphia to Harrisburg, Mr. Hone stating that it took him five days to go from the State capital to Pittsburgh—most of the way by canal boat. The stagecoaches of colonial days were still in use between many points, while in the interior river steamers— which blew up with alarming frequency—were the chief means of locomotion. The trans-Atlantic steamship record was reduced from fifteen days to eleven in 1840 by the *Acadia,* which remained the queen of the early ocean greyhounds until 1848.

In 1841 the epoch-making invention of the magnetic telegraph was still in its infancy. It was first announced to the public in April, 1837, its inventor modestly stating that he "presumed that five words could be transmitted in a minute." It was seven years,

2

however, before the first telegraph line in the United States was completed—that between Washington and Baltimore. It was not until 1866 that the first Atlantic cable was laid, while the telephone was given to the world ten years later. Postal facilities were equally primitive. In 1840 the first national postage stamps were issued in Great Britain—an improvement t h a t was not adopted over here until 1847; while it was 1856 before prepayment of postage was made compulsory by law in this country.

During the first three or four decades of the nation's history there w a s a k e e n rivalry between New York, Boston a n d Philadelphia a s t o which should become the commercial metropolis of the Republic. The contest was virtually settled by the completion of

The first Merchants' Exchange, situated on Wall Street
(From an engraving published in 1830)

the Erie Canal in 1825, and during the next decade New York grew very rapidly. The canal made the city the chief port of shipment for the products of the interior and the leading distributing center for imported merchandise. Great trading houses sprang up, having connections with retail merchants in all parts of the country. In 1835 a fire destroyed almost the entire mercantile district, sweeping over an area of fifty acres, but the merchants immediately rebuilt

Ruins of the Merchants' Exchange after the great fire of December 16th and 17th, 1835

(From a contemporary print)

their ruined premises on a larger and more lavish scale than before, relying largely on European credits and liberal bank loans to do so.

At that period it was customary for western and southern traders to visit the eastern wholesale merchants and manufacturers twice a year to make their purchases in person. The terms of sale were very simple. The buyer agreed to pay for the goods purchased when he came again. In other words, the pre-

vailing system was six months' credit on all transactions. If a firm had just started in business its
buying partner brought with him—on his first visit to
the eastern jobbers—letters of recommendation from
other merchants in his vicinity, these letters being
addressed to the houses from which the merchants
were themselves purchasing and to whom they were
well known. This was the system that had existed

*The new Merchants' Exchange, "the finest mercantile edifice
in America," as it appeared in 1841*
(From a contemporary engraving)

from colonial times, but as the country expanded it
showed an increasing tendency to break down. Means
of travel and communication were slow and uncertain, and if the letter of introduction failed to convey
sufficient information upon which to extend credit
with safety weeks might elapse before it could be supplemented. Meanwhile, of course, the buyer would
go elsewhere for his goods, and a valuable account
might be lost. Moreover, after once having established trade relations on a credit basis, the jobber had

little or no means of judging whether the affairs of his customer were prospering or the reverse. Periods of depression occurred with great frequency in which the eastern sellers lost heavily, owing to the inability of western and southern buyers to meet their obligations. Some of these retail failures were caused by crop shortages, others by money stringency, but the greater proportion were due to the fact that credit had been injudiciously extended to traders who were not entitled to it. A most striking instance of the extremely high rate of mercantile mortality resulting from this unsound method of granting credits is given by Lewis Tappan, the founder of The Mercantile Agency, in an Appendix to his *Life of Arthur Tappan*:

In 1832 a clergyman came to New York to solicit funds for a college in Missouri. A loan of $10,000 was finally obtained on the following terms: (1) That the trustees of the college should mortgage to the lender, as security for their bond, the land to be purchased from the United States; (2) that forty merchants in New York, who had expressed a willingness to loan their names to the amount of $500 each, should unite in a guaranty; (3) that five of the number give a bond indorsing the responsibility of the forty; (4) that the friend who negotiated the loan on behalf of the institution should give his obligation to hold the lender harmless at all events, or, in other words, to repay the sum advanced if the others did not. At the end of ten years, when the loan became due, the trustees were unable to repay it. No. 4 was then applied to, but did not have the means to meet the obligation. Of the five merchants in No. 3 four had become insolvent. The only solvent one among them then endeavored to collect their respective quotas from the forty merchants in No. 2, but found that a large portion of these had also failed, so that he was compelled to settle with the lender himself. When the loan was made, those in the No. 2 list were all in prosperous circumstances, and each of the No. 3 list was rich. Yet, such were the uncertainties of trade under the credit system which then prevailed, that in less than ten years nearly all of these merchants had become bankrupts.

The prevailing system of long-term credits, based upon very insufficient information as to the buyer's responsibility in most instances, was one of the chief causes of the great panic of 1837, and contributed

The Park and City Hall, New York, as they appeared in 1841, when The Mercantile Agency was established

(From an engraving published in 1838)

especially to the extraordinarily high number of failures that occurred among strictly mercantile houses during that crisis and the periods of severe depression that succeeded it in 1839 and 1840. Other causes of the disaster of 1837 were speculation in Government lands, inflation of bank loans, unsound currency, over-

expansion of trade, and serious crop failures—a group
of adverse factors sufficiently formidable to wreck
almost any country. New highways, railroads and
canals had opened up immense areas of previously
inaccessible lands that were sold by the Government
on easy terms—$1.25 per acre, payable in any kind
of currency. As the market value of these lands
quickly rose above the Government's prices, an era
of land speculation set in that greatly overdiscounted
the immediate future. Local banks loaned freely on
newly purchased and unimproved Government lands,
and new banks were established to meet this tempo-
rary demand. In 1829 the number of banks in the
country was 329, and the total loans aggregated $137,-
000,000. In 1837 the number of banks was 788 and
the aggregate of loans $525,100,000. Much of this
inflation in loans was based on unimproved lands in
the hands of speculators.

The money in circulation at this period consisted
almost entirely of paper, with very little gold or silver behind it. The bank notes of many of the States
were not current in other States. Counterfeits were
numerous, and "Counterfeit Bank Note Detectors"
were in almost universal use among merchants and
others receiving paper money. "No one was safe
without them—nor especially safe with them," according to a merchant of that period. A currency so
essentially unsound became a menace whenever business conditions were disturbed.

As stated, causes of disturbance were not lacking in **1837**. The mania for speculation was not confined to western lands. Prices of cotton plantations,

Wall Street as it appeared in 1849, a few years after The Mercantile Agency was established. The building at the right is still standing

especially in Mississippi and Louisiana, rose sharply, as did prices of real estate in southern cities. At Mobile, for example, the assessed value of real estate rose from $1,250,000 in 1834 to $27,000,000 in 1837. Prices of cotton were soaring. The famous Specie Circular issued by the United States Treasury Department in 1836 pricked the western land bubble by requiring that agents for the sale of public lands should accept only specie and refuse bank notes of all kinds. At the same time a number of failures in Great Britain compelled houses there to call their American loans, which caused a heavy fall in cotton and crippled the South. The crop failures of 1835 and 1837 affected the merchants adversely in the farming sections of the North and West. At this moment, when the business community was confronted by the most serious crisis in the history of the country, the Treasury Department called upon the banks holding national funds for $9,000,000 as a first payment of the surplus to be distributed among the States. "Millions of dollars went on their travels North and South, East and West, being mere freight for the time being, while the business from which the money was withdrawn gasped for breath in its struggle with a fearfully stringent money market."* This was in January, 1837. On April 1st a second installment was called for, but the sorely pressed banks were not equal to the strain.

On May 10th the banks of New York City suspended specie payments, followed the next day by the banks in many other cities. As was to be expected, security prices fell during the first months of the year

---

* Carl Schurz, Life of Henry Clay.

to less than half, in many instances, of the prices of the year before. Real estate prices at New York declined even more sharply. Lots at Bloomingdale (near 100th Street), which cost $480 each the previous September, were sold at $50. Real estate throughout the city depreciated more than $40,000,000 in six months. In two months there were over 250 failures, while the value of merchandise stocks on

Wall Street from the corner of Broad Street. From a print published about the time that this section began to be known as the financial district

hand in warehouses and stores declined 30 per cent. The situation throughout the country was the same. All banks suspended specie payments, and the total number of failures among mercantile houses has never been reported. In proportion to the number of firms in business it was probably the largest in the history of the country.

Among the more notable failures was that of Arthur Tappan & Co., wholesale and retail silk dealers, whose establishment on Pearl Street at Hanover Square (then the heart of the fashionable shopping district), was one of the largest in the country, with sales amounting to over a million dollars per annum. With Arthur Tappan was associated his brother Lewis, who had charge of the credits of the firm. At the outset the partners proposed to sell only for cash, but "the general practice of merchants at that day, the earnest solicitations of customers, the temptations to sell at greater profits, and the apparent success of the credit system, influenced the firm to depart, by degrees, from the rule that had been established until its principal sales were made on credit."*

Few houses, even in those days, had stricter rules for their employees than those laid down by Arthur Tappan & Co. They were required: (1) To be strictly temperate; (2) to avoid fast habits and bad companions; (3) to keep away from theaters; (4) to attend Divine service twice on the Sabbath Day; (5) to report at the store every Monday morning what church they had attended, the name of the clergyman and the text; (6) to attend prayer-meetings twice a week, and (7) never to be out after 10 o'clock P. M.†

In determining credits the brothers were equally exacting. Each applicant was questioned individually, usually by Lewis, and no detail reported was ever forgotten—both brothers being noted for their

* Life of Arthur Tappan.
† The Old Merchants of New York City.

very retentive memories. In this manner the firm gradually accumulated a large amount of information regarding buyers in all parts of the country. As an instance of the high esteem with which their fellow merchants regarded the Tappans as credit authorities, A. T. Stewart, in the early stages of his career— when doubts were expressed as to whether he was going beyond his resources—named Lewis Tappan "as a fit and proper person, both from integrity and business shrewdness, to look into his accounts and make an impartial report of his pecuniary condition, so as to set all doubts at rest." During the early thirties, as the extent and reliability of the information they had accumulated for their own use became generally known, Arthur Tappan & Co. were frequently consulted by fellow merchants on the subject of credits, and gave their advice freely whenever requested to do so.

The immediate cause of the Tappan failure was the fact that the firm was carrying a very heavy stock of goods at a time of great financial embarrassment. "The expansion of trade much beyond the actual wants of the country, the extensive credits given by merchants, the failure of southern traders to fulfill their engagements, added to the severe losses by fire, and other causes, were rapidly bringing on general bankruptcy," wrote Lewis Tappan in his account of the failure. The firm suspended in May, 1837, its liabilities amounting to $1,100,000. The creditors were given notes for six, twelve and eighteen months in lieu of their claims. These were paid promptly as they came due, but business conditions continuing to be unsatisfactory, Lewis soon afterward retired from the firm, followed by Arthur in 1840, the business passing to other hands.

The panic of 1837 has been described in some detail because it not only led directly to the establishment of The Mercantile Agency, but was largely responsible for its early success. The failure of A. Tappan & Co. left Lewis, its credit manager, free to engage in some new occupation. His wide experience in appraising the credit responsibility of traders, and the high regard in which his opinions on credits were held by other wholesale merchants, suggested the idea of organizing a credit reporting bureau devoted to collecting and disseminating such information for the benefit of the mercantile community as a whole. The great lesson of the panic, as he saw it—after studying closely its causes and effects—was that the system of mercantile credits that had prevailed until then was essentially unsound because it failed to take sufficiently into account the standing of the applicant for credit, based upon information obtained from intelligent and reliable sources. Likewise, the panic, with its overthrow of merchants and traders of every grade of credit reputation from the lowest to the highest, had convinced business men generally that there was something wrong with a system that could result in so universal a collapse. They were, therefore, quick to perceive the need of an institution for safeguarding credits by enabling the seller to inform himself more exactly regarding the character and standing of each applicant.

LEWIS TAPPAN
The founder of The Mercantile Agency
(From an engraving in *America's Advancement,* published in 1875)

Encouraged by the result of the inquiries he had made among his fellow merchants as to the favor with which they would regard his novel enterprise, Lewis Tappan determined to establish what he called "The

15

Mercantile Agency" in the year 1841. On June 1st
of that year he sent an announcement of his project
to all of the leading merchants of New York City,
and especially to those engaged in the wholesale trade
with merchants in other parts of the country—"in the
country trade," as people called it in those days. In
this announcement Mr. Tappan set August 1st as
the date for beginning active operations, and on that
day the new institution—the first of its kind in the
world—opened its doors for the transaction of business under the name of The Mercantile Agency, which
it has ever since retained. The first place of business
was at the corner of Hanover Street and Exchange
Place, close to the store of A. Tappan & Co. (the successors of Arthur and Lewis Tappan).

The months of June and July were evidently
spent in securing subscribers to the new Agency.
The original subscription book used by Lewis Tappan is still in existence. It is a little pocket memo-
randum book, six inches high by about four wide,
covered with imitation leather. On the first page
Mr. Tappan wrote the terms of the first Agency contract, which were as follows:

> We the subscribers, individuals and firms, trad-
> ing and selling merchandise in the City of New York,
> being acquainted with the objects of The Mercantile
> Agency as set forth in a published Circular signed by
> Lewis Tappan, approving thereof and being desirous
> to avail ourselves of its advantages, do hereby sev-
> erally agree to pay to the said Lewis Tappan, for the
> information which he may be able to furnish us from
> time to time at the office of said Agency for one year
> from the first day of August, 1841, and until we shall

inform said Tappan in writing of our wish to discontinue our subscriptions—three months notice thereof to be given—the sums of money which shall be payable by us respectively in advance according to the following terms, to wit:

Those of us whose sales of goods for one year amount to One Hundred Thousand dollars or less will severally and respectively pay One Hundred dollars.

Those whose sales are over $100,000 and less than $200,000, One Hundred and fifty dollars.

Those whose sales are over $200,000 and less than $350,000, Two Hundred dollars.

Those whose sales are over $350,000 and less than $500,000, Two Hundred and fifty dollars.

And all whose sales are over $500,000, Three Hundred dollars.

And the subscribers do further agree and promise to send all their claims that are or shall be past due, and for the collection or settlement of which they need the agency of another person, to the correspondents of said Tappan, it being understood that said correspondents shall do the business as promptly and faithfully as other attorneys and agents, and that their charges and commissions shall be at the customary rates.

July 31, 1841.

After so prolonged a period of uncertainty and disaster—for the panic of 1837 was followed by similar, though less intense periods of depression in 1839 and 1840—merchants were ready to welcome any plan that gave promise of increased safety, and the solicitors of the new organization met with the most flattering success. When the new Agency was opened for business, Mr. Tappan's first step was to issue a circular to lawyers and others inviting them to become his correspondents. In this way he hoped to be able to secure, *in advance,* sufficient data regarding the standing of traders to enable merchants to whom they might subsequently apply for credit to deter-

17

[facsimile of handwritten signatures]

1. *[signature]*
2. A. Tappan & Co.
3. *[signature]*
4. *[signature]*
5. *[signature]*
6. Benj. D. Godfrey

[additional handwritten signatures]

60 Maiden Lane

The first page of signatures to the original subscription book of The Mercantile Agency, dated July 31st, 1841

mine what amount of credit, if any, could safely be accorded to them. His own experience, as dispenser of credits for Arthur Tappan & Co., had taught him that after the buyer arrived and presented his letters of introduction and recommendation, the seller was in possession of only a part of the information he required in order to arrive at a safe decision. Obvi-

Exchange Place, looking toward Hanover Street. The first office of The Mercantile Agency was at the corner of Exchange Place and Hanover Street; the second at No. 9 Exchange Place

ously, no man would refer him to those who knew any ill of him, while letters of introduction might be furnished by those who gave them merely to avoid the unpleasant necessity of explaining to the credit applicant in person why they refused to do so. The responses to the preliminary circular proved satisfactory, and The Mercantile Agency rapidly accumulated a valuable mass of reports. These were written in longhand—the invention of the typewriter was still many years in the future—in huge ledgers bound in sheepskin. The present proprietors of The Mercantile Agency, R. G. DUN & Co., still have these primitive report books of the forties and fifties among their archives. It would indeed be difficult to surpass the beauty of the handwriting in many of these reports in this modern stenographic and typewriter age.

Almost from the very outset, it became increasingly apparent that the service of the new institution would be greatly improved, and the number of subscribers correspondingly increased, if branch offices were opened in the principal cities. Accordingly, in February, 1843, Mr. Tappan proposed to Edward E. Dunbar, a Boston business man, that he open a branch of The Mercantile Agency in that city, which was done almost immediately under the firm style of Edward E. Dunbar & Co., Mr. Tappan and Mr. Dunbar each taking a half interest. Speaking a little later of his early experiences in opening the office, Mr. Dunbar wrote:

> The enterprise was entirely new to Boston merchants. Some were aware that a concern of this kind had been established in New York, but they were almost wholly unacquainted with its practical operation and uses. I had neither the countenance of my friends nor the confidence of merchants in my novel, or, as many regarded it, mysterious undertaking. It was a long

time before they could be brought to see that my object was simply to collect useful information respecting trade and traders all over the country, by means of special agents and an organized correspondence of lawyers, for the benefit of merchants in the city who sold goods to persons in the country; and to afford facilities for the collection of debts by keeping a registry of prompt and faithful attorneys throughout the United States who would obtain information and correspond with the Agency.

For several months Mr. Dunbar labored arduously, but made little apparent progress. He then received the following letter from Mr. Tappan:

I am beginning to think seriously whether it is not for my interest to invite you to give up the branch at Boston and unite with me here. Were you here this fall, or, rather, had you been here the first of August, I could have secured a large number of new subscribers and have greatly strengthened my system.

To this Mr. Dunbar replied, on September 5th, 1843, in part, as follows:

First, respecting the Agency here. That we will ultimately succeed I feel confident. . . . I take the broad ground that the institution is founded on good principles and that its operation and effect are of immense benefit to the community, and it is only necessary for the community to see this in order to support it. It requires a longer time to operate on public opinion in Boston than in New York. I have broken ground here and certainly accomplished much in doing away with the prejudice, and inducing the community to view the system impartially. The trade of the West is turning this way in such a manner that by and by the necessity of such an institution cannot but be apparent to the merchants. Time, labor and money have been expended—the foundation is laid. The system is organized and offered to merchants for their examination and use. . . . Had I now a direct pecuniary interest in the New York office I think I should be willing to incur some expense in maintaining the Agency here, for the following reasons, viz.:

First. The great influence that is brought to bear in favor of the New York office, as my arrangements with correspondents have been effected, to a great extent, on account of my connection with that office.

Second. Much valuable information is obtained by the Agency here that is adapted to New York, which the office there must in any case obtain.

The Boston Office, established 1843
This office has for many years been located at No. 3 Winthrop
Square, where it occupies the entire second floor

Third. Should the Agency here be given up, perhaps someone else would establish one, and take the benefit of my labors.

Fourth. Should this Agency be suddenly brought to an end, it would have a bad effect on the New York office.

These cogent arguments evidently convinced Mr. Tappan of the importance of continuing the Boston office, and in the spring of 1844 the business of the new branch began to increase. On March 1st, Mr. Dunbar purchased Mr. Tappan's interest in the Boston office, and by July 1st, the income of the branch exceeded expenses. On this date Mr. Dunbar sold half of his interest in the Boston office and, at the request of Mr. Tappan, went to New York, where he purchased a fourth interest in the head

A corner of the Boston Office
In every office the cases in which the Agency's records are kept form a prominent feature

office for $7,500, the establishment then being valued at $30,000. The firm name remained, as before, Lewis Tappan & Co.

In October, 1844, Charles Barlow entered the employ of The Mercantile Agency, as copyist and correspondence clerk. Mr. Barlow was born in Dudley, England, in 1820; and came to the United States

at the age of twenty, first obtaining employment with
A. T. Stewart. He remained in the service of the
Agency until his death, in 1880, at which time he was
one of the partners of the firm.

The next branch office to be established was that
at Philadelphia, which was opened July 2nd, 1845,
under the firm style of William Goodrich & Co. The
partners were Wil-
liam Goodrich, a
highly trusted em-
ployee of L e w i s
Tappan & Co., and
Edward E. Dunbar.
It was agreed that
Mr. Tappan should
receive a certain sum
out of the profits in
return for relinquish-
ing the partnership
a n d affording the
new branch access to
all the information
received a t N e w

Philadelphia Office, established 1845
Occupying all of the 13th and most of the
12th floors of the Lincoln Building

York. Within six months the success of the new
office was assured, while New York and Boston were
supplied with full and thorough reports from a large
section of the country that had previously been inade-
quately reported, and the number of correspondents
throughout the region greatly increased. During the
fall of 1845, Messrs. Goodrich and Dunbar urged the

importance of opening a new office at Baltimore, as the South was then the great market for manufactures and imports of all kinds, and it was there that reliable credit reports were most urgently needed. The West was then of relatively little commercial importance, Chicago having a population of only 4,470, while St. Louis was a bustling little frontier river port and fur-trade center with 16,-469 inhabitants. Accordingly, early in 1846, an office was opened at Baltimore in charge of Jabez D. Pratt, the firm style being J. D. Pratt & Co. The new office had the entire South for its district, and

Baltimore Office, established 1846
This office occupies the entire sixth floor
of the Maryland Trust Building

therefore soon became one of the most important links in the Agency's chain.

In 1843, when the first branch office was opened at Boston the number of correspondents of the Agency was about 180, the list covering part of New England and the States of New York, New Jersey, Pennsylvania, Ohio, Michigan, Indiana, Illinois, Iowa and Wisconsin. By 1846 the number of correspondents of the New York office was 352, of the Boston office 115, and the Philadelphia office 212—or 679 altogether, not including those of the new Baltimore office which had just been organized. The Mercantile Agency was then five years old, its business was firmly established and all of its branches were prospering. As important changes in its management took place during the year 1846 that date may fairly be taken as indicating the end of the period of inception, when the plans and policies of the youthful and novel institution were necessarily more or less formative, and the beginning of the period during which the fundamental characteristics of The Mercantile Agency of to-day were clearly determined.

CHAPTER II

The Development of the Mercantile Agency Idea

1846–1854

⟨>∘⊠∘<⟩

EARLY in the year 1846 increasing differences
of opinion between Mr. Tappan and Mr. Dunbar
as to the manner in which the business of The Mercantile Agency should be conducted resulted in a
dissolution of the partnership, Mr. Tappan purchasing Mr. Dunbar's interest in the New York office,
and the late junior partner agreeing "not to engage
in the mercantile agency or any similar business prior
to July 1st, 1849." On December 31st, Mr. Dunbar
went to California, selling his interest in the Philadelphia office to Mr. Goodrich, and that in the Boston office to George William Gordon, who had previously been Postmaster at Boston and Consul General at Rio de Janeiro. Mr. Dunbar's retirement
from the business left Mr. Tappan in sole charge
of the management of the parent institution at
New York—a responsibility that his advancing age
and huge personal correspondence made very irk-
some to him.

About June, 1846, Mr. Tappan made the acquaintance of Benjamin Douglass, the eldest son of
George Douglass, who for many years had been a

27

successful West India merchant at Baltimore, Md., and later at New York. After being associated in business with his father for a number of years, Benjamin Douglass went to Charleston, S. C., conducting an extensive mercantile business there for some time, and then removed to New Orleans, where he extended his trade to all parts of the Mississippi Valley. It was his habit to investigate the credit standing of his customers in person, making extensive trips for that purpose throughout the South and Southwest, and even as far north as the State of Ohio. Although only thirty years old at this time, Mr. Douglass was, therefore, very familiar with the business methods in the "country trade," and with the loose system of granting credits to country buyers that was then customary. This experience enabled him to appreciate clearly the importance and value of the mercantile agency idea.

Perceiving that the unusually wide family and business connections of Mr. Douglass would be of inestimable service in securing for The Mercantile Agency the support of the South, Mr. Tappan offered the young man a position in his establishment as confidential clerk and secretary. Mr. Douglass had hardly been in the office two weeks before he proposed to Mr. Tappan that he be allowed to take charge of all correspondence relating to the Agency, thus leaving his employer free to devote his time to his private correspondence. This proposition the elder man accepted gladly, and the new associate be-

came at once head clerk and the virtual manager of
the business, which—as a result of his diligence and
skill—quickly began to improve.   In **1847** Mr. Doug-

From a painting in the possession of R. G. DUN & Co.
BENJAMIN DOUGLASS
*Part owner of The Mercantile Agency from 1847 to 1854, and sole
proprietor from 1854 to 1859*

lass acquired a third interest in the Agency, Mr. Tappan retaining the other two-thirds. Benjamin Doug-

lass was a man of commanding personality, of iron will and inflexible loyalty to principle, and under his direction The Mercantile Agency began to develop along broader and stronger lines.

The first result of the new spirit injected into the management of the business was a marked strengthening of the firm's system of correspondents in the South. Mr. Douglass earnestly advocated the opening of new offices in the South and West, clearly perceiving that the success of the business must ultimately depend upon the extent and thoroughness of its facilities for ascertaining the standing of merchants and traders in all sections of the country. While no new offices were opened in 1847 and 1848 the list of correspondents was greatly extended. The Philadelphia office reached out as far westward as Pittsburgh, while the service of the Baltimore branch covered the entire South to New Orleans. Mr. James H. Taylor, an employee of the Philadelphia office from 1847 until 1911—a period of sixty-four years—in an interesting account of the early history of the Agency in that city wrote:

> Every morning we received a package of letters from New York City and from Baltimore, Md., by the Adams Express, containing reports in our district or that we were interested in, for us to copy and return, while we daily sent a package of reports that we had received and written up to these offices. . . . As I was noted for having a tenacious memory, Mr. Goodrich would send me to various leading firms, instructing me to ask them what they knew about the parties inquired for, giving me orders to listen attentively to what they

said and remember the conversation, bring it back and
write it up, which I did, and that was the basis of our
city reporting.

On June 1st, 1849, Lewis Tappan retired from
The Mercantile Agency, which up to that time had
been known as Lewis Tappan & Co.   He was succeeded by his brother, Arthur Tappan, and Benjamin Douglass, each of whom purchased a half interest in the business.   As Lewis Tappan never again
took an active part in the great institution he

New York City about 1855
Showing the shipping in the East River—sailing vessels still pre-
dominating—and the low sky line of Manhattan Island

founded, it is fitting at this point to review briefly his
work in the early years of its inception and organization.   That he was the originator and founder of
the first organized system of credit reporting in the
world has never been disputed.   This fact is strongly
emphasized by the author of the sketch of Lewis Tap-

pan in *America's Advancement,* published in 1875, a
portion of which follows:

> We have introduced the name and portrait of Mr.
> Tappan into this work because he is identified with a
> very important movement in the mercantile world, which
> may almost be said to have revolutionized the method of
> conducting business, especially as regards dispensing
> credits. We refer to The Mercantile Agency and the
> system pursued under that name. He was, during his
> lifetime, it is true, identified with many other very im-
> portant movements, and was very actively instrumental
> in carrying them forward. . . . But of the mercantile
> agency system, he may fairly be called the originator,
> or father.
>
> Mr. Tappan impressed upon The Mercantile Agency
> his peculiar characteristics almost as clearly as John
> Wesley did his upon Methodism; and, although various
> adaptations and modifications have been necessary to
> meet the exigencies of business, these peculiarities are
> still clearly discernible. He had many enemies and
> many admirers during his lifetime, as men of strong
> will and purpose are apt to have; but no one ever
> doubted his perfect honesty and fair-mindedness, and
> his desire to give to every man his just due.
>
> We have said that Mr. Tappan was the originator
> and father of the mercantile agency system. We be-
> lieve we are justified in using these terms. Some crude
> attempts had been made, it is true, at something which
> was intended to supply what the Agency supplies, before
> his time; but they had never been brought to any practi-
> cal results; and, indeed, may be said to have been aban-
> doned when Mr. Tappan entered the field. The idea
> suggested itself to him from a long experience of his
> own in business, and a knowledge of the difficulty, which
> all dispensers of credit experienced at that time, in
> obtaining anything like tangible information on which
> to operate. While in the house of Arthur Tappan &
> Co.—then the leading dry-goods firm in New York—
> and engaged in dispensing its credits, he had little to
> go upon except such information as could be gained
> from other houses to which he was referred by the par-

ties themselves, or from open letters of introduction or recommendation which the applicants brought with them from some influential source at home, and which were supplied generally at their own request. . . . The fact is, that credits given under this system very nearly resembled what Sir Astley Cooper said of surgical operations before his time, viz., that "they were a series of doubtful experiments." We seriously question whether a system which so completely revolutionized all ideas of business usages and traditions could have been successfully carried out under any other person. At least, we are quite sure that there are very few persons who could have done it. Mr. Tappan, in the first place, was a man well known in the community. His business ability was almost universally recognized. . . . In short, his acknowledged business shrewdness, his incorruptible integrity, and the fact that his own experience as a dispenser of credits had prompted him to attempt something that should obviate the perplexities he had himself felt, were all strong arguments in favor of a movement in the direction proposed by The Mercantile Agency, and it is difficult to imagine any other person in whom all these considerations were combined in the same degree. . . .

Mr. Tappan lived long enough to see the tree that he planted grown to proportions and yielding fruit far beyond what he himself probably anticipated; and we doubt whether among all the movements and enterprises with which he was identified, he will find as lasting a memorial, or as distinct a recognition, as in The Mercantile Agency, destined, probably, to live as long as commerce or civilization, and to carry with it the name of its founder, as one of the far-seeing and original minds which have impressed themselves upon the history, development and prosperity of their country.

No finer or juster tribute to the genius of the founder of The Mercantile Agency has ever been written than this, and the forty years that have since elapsed only serve still further to emphasize its truth.

Lewis Tappan lived until 1873, his last work being the preparation of a life of his brother Arthur, which was published in 1870. In 1827 he founded the *New York Journal of Commerce,* which has been published continuously ever since.

Cincinnati Office, established 1849
The present office is located in the First
National Bank Building

The style of the firm on the retirement of Lewis Tappan was changed to Tappan & Douglass, A r t h u r Tappan becoming the senior partner under an a g r e e m e n t by which he contracted to leave the business in the sole proprietorship of his associate at the end of five years. To the men in the service of the Agency, Mr. Douglass w a s looked upon as the guiding spirit of the institution and his influence a n d strong personality now began to modify its policies materially. Arthur Tappan was sixty-three years old, and it was the younger partner who traveled to all parts of the country to extend and strengthen the service of the Agency, and who fought its battles. In 1849,

Mr. Douglass opened a branch of The Mercantile
Agency at Cincinnati, which was then the great metropolis of the western trade, with a population of
115,435. The office was operated by William B.
Pierce and Samuel Richardson, under the firm style
of Wm. B. Pierce & Co. The new venture was so

Louisville Office, established 1850
Main room of the present office in the Board of Trade Building.
There are five other rooms occupied by the Agency

successful that the following year Wm. B. Pierce &
Co. opened an office at Louisville, the sixth in the
Agency's chain. While, during this period, the plan
of giving the new offices separate firm styles inaugurated by Lewis Tappan was continued, Mr. Douglass made it clear that every office must be subordi-

nate to that at New York, where the policies of the institution were decided.

In 1850 an office was opened at St. Louis. At that time the trading station of ten years before had expanded into a roaring hive of frontier industry and commerce. Long lines of steamers clung to the levee along the river front and the merchandise received and distributed bore the names of traders throughout the vast region drained by the Mississippi and its tributaries — an empire for one Mercantile Agency district. The new office was opened by Charles Barlow, who remained in charge until 1854, when the new branch was thoroughly established and its success assured. The firm style at the outset was

St. Louis Office, established 1850
*The present office is located in Mechanics-
American National Bank Building*

Charles Barlow & Co. Among the first correspondents of the St. Louis office was Abraham Lincoln, then a successful attorney at Springfield, in the part of Illinois falling within the St. Louis district. The quaint humor that enlivened so many of the future

President's public utterances was not absent from
his reports to The Mercantile Agency.

The archives of the St. Louis office still contain
records showing many reports written by Mr. Lincoln on some of the oldest and largest concerns in
the State of Illinois during those early days. Nor
was he the only correspondent who subsequently
achieved fame in professional or public life. Many of
the offices have on their rolls of correspondents

*A view of a portion of the St. Louis office,
which occupies 12,500 square feet of floor space, and is entirely
modern throughout*

the names of judges in the highest courts of their
respective States and in the courts of the United
States; while scores of the correspondents of the
various offices have since become Governors, members of the United States Senate and House of Representatives, and of State Legislatures. This, indeed, was only natural, since the aim of the Agency
has always been to enlist the services and secure the
opinions of the most representative men in every

community—and these were naturally the ones most likely to be selected by their fellow citizens for political advancement. It may be of interest to add, in this connection, that ex-Presidents Arthur, Cleveland and McKinley were also associated with the work of the Agency prior to their elevation to the highest office in the gift of their countrymen.

At some time during the year 1851 a new employee entered the service of The Mercantile Agency at New York who was destined to play a most prominent part in its future development. This was Robert Graham Dun, whose name the great institution now bears. Mr. Dun was born at Chillicothe, Ohio, August 7th, 1826, of Scotch parentage. His grandfather was the Rev. James Dun, for twenty years a minister of the Free Church of Scotland at Glasgow. In 1815 his father, Robert Dun, who had also been educated for the ministry, emigrated to the United States and settled at Chillicothe. The trips made by Mr. Douglass to Ohio while he was a merchant at New Orleans may have been the indirect cause of Mr. Dun entering the service of the Agency, for at that time he met Miss Elizabeth Dun, a sister of Robert G. Dun, whom he subsequently married. By a remarkable coincidence Mr. Douglass also had a sister named Elizabeth, who married Mr. Dun. It was, in all probability, this relationship by marriage that directed the attention of Mr. Douglass to the advantages of bringing the young Ohioan to New York to assist him in the management of the business. He was himself obliged to take long and frequent trips to distant offices, and there were a number of reasons why he wished to leave in his stead at New York someone in whose integrity, good judgment and personal loyalty he could absolutely rely. The fact that the life-long friendship between the two men was never for a moment interrupted clearly proves that he found these qualities combined in his young brother-in-law to a remarkable degree. One reason, in particular, why a loyal assistant was needed at this time was the approaching retirement of Mr. Tappan from the Agency. Certain of the older employees of the Tappans, being aware of the impending change, were taking steps to continue their respective branches as independent concerns, while Mr. Douglass aimed to keep the organization together. By his diligence in mastering the principles of the mercantile agency business, and his watchfulness in safeguarding the interests entrusted to his care, Mr. Dun quickly won the complete confidence of Mr. Douglass, nor was he long in winning the esteem of the mercantile community at New York.

Early in 1851 Mr. Gordon, the head of the Boston office of The Mercantile Agency, was again appointed Postmaster of that city, and accordingly sold his interest in the business to Edward Russell. The firm style at Boston was therefore changed to Edward Russell & Co.—under which name that branch of the business continued to be conducted for almost half a century.

In June, 1851, The Mercantile Agency had completed the first decade of its existence. The business community in every city in which a branch office had been opened thus far had been quick to recognize the importance and value of the new institution and had given it a generous measure of support. Fortunately a contemporary picture of the activities of the Agency at this period of its development has come down to us in the form of an article that appeared in the January, 1851, number of *Hunt's Merchants' Magazine and Commercial Review,* and bears every evidence of having been written by Freeman Hunt himself. The following extracts from this article are of particular interest as showing how the first Mercantile Agency in the world was regarded by the public when it was ten years old.

THE MERCANTILE AGENCY

This institution, which has now been many years in operation, has grown to be so important to the mercantile community that we feel it due to our subscribers to notice it in our pages. . . . Our present remarks, while they are intended to cover the *system,* have reference more particularly to the oldest and most extensive of these agencies, conducted by Messrs. Tappan & Douglass, which we have personally inspected.

This is not only an extensive, influential, and, as we believe, useful institution in New York, but is extended by associate offices to Boston, Philadelphia, Baltimore, Cincinnati, St. Louis and Louisville; and contemplates a still further extension, so as to embrace all the important centers of trade in the United States. But, though known and appreciated by a majority of the merchants in the large cities, we are aware that a prejudice exists against it in some quarters. Our object is, if possible, to remove that prejudice, by presenting the matter to our readers in the light in which it now appears to us. We say *now,* for we are free to acknowledge that our own "first impressions" were unfavorable. On a full examination of the subject, however, we are convinced that those impressions were founded in ignorance of the system. We have recently taken pains to inform ourselves, and do not hesitate to say, that the Agency is conducted on high and honorable principles, and is truly and extensively useful, not only to the city merchants, for whose immediate benefit it was devised and established, but to all sound, upright, industrious traders throughout the land.

In our review of this system, we shall briefly advert, first to the *object* of the mercantile agencies, and then to their *operations.*

And, first, as to their object. Immediately after the terrible mercantile revolution in 1837, when our whole system of internal commerce was prostrate, and nearly all its operators bankrupt, this Agency was planned, and put into operation, as a remedy for some of the difficulties which had just been so heavily experienced. Its design was to uphold, extend, and render safe and profitable to all concerned, the great credit system, on which our country had thriven, doing business to an immense amount with all the world, and using the capital of the world to do it with.

At the outset it was mainly intended as an aid to the *Jobber.* His customers, scattered over many States, were periodically visiting him for the purpose of renewing their stocks of goods; generally canceling in whole, or in part, previous obligations, while they contracted new ones. The intelligent jobber would necessarily need to be informed, on the opening of a new account, respecting the then circumstances of his customer. From year to year he would desire to be freshly advised of the good or ill success attending him.

To carry out the credit system, intelligently and safely, the creditor must be well acquainted with the debtor's financial condition and general standing. Confidence is the life of the system, and confidence can rest only in knowledge. Before the establishment of this Agency our merchants were in the habit of getting such information of their customers as they could, by correspondence or otherwise. Some of the larger houses, whose business would justify the expense, employed traveling agents. These' they kept constantly out, in different parts of the country, looking after and reporting their debtors, and collecting debts. The smaller houses were, of course, deficient in the knowledge so necessary to their success in business, while the larger ones purchased their information at too high a cost. The Agency obviates these difficulties. By an extensive and well-sustained system of correspondents, extending to every part of the United States and Canada, it obtains the requisite information respecting every trader in the country whose business leads him to contract debts away from home. This information is copied in books prepared for the purpose, and held for the use of such merchants as pay for it, and want it. It is not made public. It is not communicated, even to subscribers, except when a trader, by soliciting credit, renders inquiry into his circumstances necessary. It is made known only to those with whom he proposes to trade. If he does not ask a credit at all, it remains on the record, unread and unseen, from year to year.

It appears, then, that the object of the system is simply to furnish the merchant subscriber with such information as will enable him to judge whether or not, and to what extent, he should give credit to parties applying for it—thereby rendering the credit system safe and profitable. . . . The rapid growth of the Agency during the past five years, its vastly increased patronage, and the increasing confidence in it by the merchants in our large cities, are sufficient proof that the reports furnished are substantially correct, and a safe guide in their credit operations. We have, also, *tested* this point on a small scale, but quite to our own satisfaction. We have inquired for parties well known to us, and found the reports, in all cases, in admirable harmony with our own opinion and knowledge of facts.

A simple inspection of the office in New York is sufficient to satisfy any man that it is largely and liberally patronized. Shrewd men do not make an expensive show of business merely for effect. Upward of thirty men are constantly occupied in the details of this office alone, condensing, copying, and giving out reports, carrying on the correspondence, etc. Their records are contained in more than 100 books, of the size of the largest ledger, extending to 600 and 700 pages each.

One other point in the operations, and one of considerable importance, remains to be noticed, and that is its effect upon the country trader. On this point, we have expressed the opinion, which is the result of deliberate examination, that the system is as useful to those who seek credit as to the city merchants who are called upon to give it. It is a well-known fact that, formerly, the trader was confined in his purchases to a few houses, where he might have formed an acquaintance. If wholly unacquainted, he was obliged to take letters from responsible parties at home, and was limited in his business relations to the few to whom those letters were addressed. Under the present arrangement, the trader needs no letter of introduction. He is known to the whole list of the Agency's subscribers, or, if not known, becomes so, as soon as he asks a credit. He has the range of the entire market in all the cities where these offices are established; the communication between them being such that what is known to one is known to all. He need not even leave home to make his purchases. His order is as good as his presence. . . . This, surely, is a great advantage, which the honest, capable, and trustworthy trader cannot fail to appreciate. We are confident, from what we have seen and learned of the workings of the system, that the instances in which it enlarges credit to the country trade are vastly more numerous than those in which it restrains or prevents it. There are, doubtless, many who, without being aware of it, are now indebted to this Agency for a good standing and a favorable position, in places, and with houses, where once they were wholly unknown. Their sphere of operations is enlarged, their business acquaintances increased, and all their facilities for conducting a profitable trade greatly extended.

A second advantage, and by no means a light one,
which the country trader derives from this system, is
the protection it affords against the unhealthy and injurious competition of fraudulent or incompetent neighbors in the same business.   There is no greater draw-
back to the success of an honest, industrious tradesman
in a small town or village, than the irregular, shuffling
transactions of a weak, lame, broken-winged or wing-
less rival, who does everything at haphazard, buying
at any price, and selling at any sacrifice, merely to keep
up a flow of business out of which he may manage to live
for the time being.   There are many grades of such
characters in the business world.   Some of them are
flagrantly dishonest, expecting and willing to fail now
and then, and resolved, at all events, to have a living
out of any whom they can surprise into trusting them.
Some, on the other hand, are well-intentioned but incompetent; without knowing why, or how, they find
themselves every now and then in failing circumstances.
These are more to be respected than the other class, but
scarcely more to be trusted.   They are as much in the
way of the capable, energetic, well-trained business
man's success as the other.   They have no rules to go
by; but provide, as they can, for each exigency as it
arises.   They never know what they are worth, or
whether they are worth anything at all.   When they
open an account, or give a note, they never know whether
they can pay it or not.   They *hope* to pay it, and in-
tend to, *if they can.*   The experience of every well-bred
merchant and trader can furnish originals for the picture.   Against the vexatious and ruinous competition of
such men, The Mercantile Agency is designed and calcu-
lated to protect them.   It would not *injure* the weak
or the unfortunate but would commend them to employ-
ments which they are capable of managing.   Trade is a
science, to which many, who would make excellent me-
chanics or agriculturists, are wholly incompetent.

A third advantage to the capable and enterprising
trader, is found in the fact that he is, by this system,
brought very near to his creditors, is as it were, always
under their eyes, and will, consequently, be stimulated to greater watchfulness, care and circumspection

in his business. He will not be so readily tempted into rash speculations or other irregular transactions, which so often result in disaster and dishonor. It is no discredit, even to an honest man, to say that he is safer under the wholesome restraints and jealous vigilance of society than he would be without them. Many a man, with the most upright intentions, and the most confident expectations of a favorable result, has been induced to invest a portion of his means, or, to speak more properly, of the means of his creditors, in some promising, but unfortunate enterprise, which he would not have touched if those creditors had been near and cognizant of the movement. Prudence is the better part, not only of valor, but of thrift; and prudence, like the other virtues, is all the better for being watched.

Under the old system, it was impossible to hold an effective check upon the imprudent speculations of good men, or the swindling speculations of bad ones. Such operations were, in general, known only to those who suffered by them; and the operators having lost credit with them, had only to begin again with some new concern, and repeat the operation. Sometimes it happened that a trader, who had run himself out with one set of creditors, would by them be palmed off upon another, as one whom they *had* trusted—the object of the introduction being to get their own pay, in full, by shifting off the debt on their friends.

On all such operations, the Agency is an admirable check. The parties reported are known, not to their present creditors only, but to all with whom they seek to open a credit. . . . Such a check we regard as decidedly salutary and wholesome, and equally so to the well-meaning and prudent trader as to his prudent creditor.

These principles appear to us so plain and palpable that they need only to be stated. If, among the class of traders, who want more credit than they find themselves able to get, any one is still disposed to object, we take leave to ask on what principles he conducts his own business at home. Does he trust anybody, and everybody, without asking a question? When a stranger comes into the neighborhood, does he open an account with him at once, and to an unlimited extent, without inquiring into his affairs? Does he think it mean, or dishonorable, to send to the place from which the stranger came, and ascertain how far he was regarded worthy of credit *there?* Does he think the former neighbors of the newcomer mean, or dishonorable, if they tell him frankly what they think, thereby securing him a good customer, or saving him from a bad one? By no means. The principle is universal. It belongs to the retail credit business as well as to the wholesale. It governs the trader, selling his hundreds or thousands, as well as the importer, in selling his tens of thousands, or millions. Confidence, as we have before said, is the life of credit, and knowledge is the life of confidence. Business cannot go on without it.

Prior to July, 1851, it was the policy of The Mercantile Agency to refrain from reporting the trade in the cities in which its offices were located. Mr. Douglass saw that this would in time create two distinct classes in the business community—those who were reported upon and those who were not. At the outset the Agency offices had been located in the cities engaged chiefly in selling to the country trade, but now the chain included several points where the traders, while sellers in their respective districts, were buyers in the eastern centers. He, accordingly, directed the various managers to report their respective cities for the benefit of the other offices.

In the fall of 1851 a branch office was opened at New Orleans, under the firm style of B. Douglass & Co. The name indicates another important change in the policy of The Mercantile Agency, namely, the discontinuance of the plan of establishing branches under the names of the various local managers. The New Orleans office was a branch of the parent company at New York and nothing more, its resident manager being simply a salaried employee, and not a partner. As a result of this new plan, which Mr. Douglass steadfastly followed thereafter, The Mercantile Agency became a nation-wide organization with a single directing executive at the head office in New York, and a uniform policy in all its branches throughout the country.

New Orleans Office, established 1851
Now occupying the second floor of the
New Orleans National Bank Building

In the closing months of 1851 the Agency encountered the most serious crisis in its brief history thus far. An action for libel had been brought against Lewis Tappan by John B. and Horace Beardsley, of Norwalk, Ohio. The suit was tried before Judge Betts of the United States District Court in the city of New York, from November 24th to December 18th, the trial attracting great public attention and being extensively reported in the New York daily papers during its progress. The question involved in this case was the fundamental one whether those who established mercantile agencies could have clerks and correspondents to aid them or not, and could be compelled to reveal who their correspondents were. The great battle of the trial took place over the latter issue. Benjamin Douglass, who had been called as a witness, was asked during the cross-examination whether in 1848 (the date of the alleged libel) Lewis Tappan had any agent or cor-

A corner of the New Orleans office
Showing a few of the cabinets in which the records are kept—
which here go back 65 years

respondent in the town of Norwalk, Ohio. After careful reflection Mr. Douglass declined to answer this question and the judge adjourned court in order to consider at length the legal authorities cited by both sides. The following morning, Tuesday, December 9th, the court denied the witness the privilege to decline. The question was thereupon repeated, and the witness again declined to answer.*

The judge, in admonishing the witness, said that he was too intelligent a man not to know that his first duty as a citizen was obedience to the law; the law required him to answer and he ought to do so. Mr. Douglass, who was evidently prepared for this demand, replied:

It is with deep regret, sir, that I feel myself driven by an imperious necessity to refuse obedience to the order of this court. My respect for you personally, aside from that due to your office, makes this action painful. I entertain the greatest respect and veneration for the laws of my country and her courts of justice; but I have maturely deliberated on this question, and feel bound to come to the conclusion to decline to answer. When I first went into the employment of Mr. Lewis Tappan, as his confidential clerk, he demanded, and I gave, a solemn pledge, under no circumstances, to disclose the names of the agents, or of any one of them, but to keep them an inviolable secret within my own breast. I have done so. I thought that Mr. Tappan had a legitimate right to demand that pledge, and that it was proper for me to give it. I did not see in my giving that pledge, that it could have an injurious effect on the public interest. I thought Mr. Tappan's business a useful one. I believed it greatly promotive of good morals and of a sound, healthy state of trade. But, sir, I am now one of the successors of Mr. Tappan in this very business, and many of his former agents are my agents, and I am now bound to them as Mr. Tappan then was, and these agents are numerous all over the country. I feel myself held by a solemn obligation to these agents, and it is in order to save myself from the disgrace and infamy, which I believe would follow me in answering this question, that I have

---

* From report of the trial in the *New York Herald* of December 12th, 1851.

resolutely determined, though very respectfully, to the court, to decline to answer, and I assure you had this court the power to deprive me of my life, and should they threaten it, I would yet fearlessly stand by and preserve intact my sacred honor. For these reasons, Judge Betts, I feel that I am fully justified before my fellow citizens, and I hope before the court, in declining to answer this question. If your honor still persists in your determination to compel me to answer, although it would be very unpleasant to be deprived of my liberty, and separated from my family, still, there is no alternative, and I have resolved to face the situation.

At the conclusion of this address the witness was committed to the Eldridge Street Jail, for contempt of court, where he remained twenty days. The judge allowed him to be confined in the house in front of the jail, but a part of it. He had a room on the first floor, where he carried on business as if he were in his own office, messengers going to and fro every day. The trial continued until December 18th, resulting in a verdict for the plaintiff. On appeal to the United States Circuit Court this judgment was affirmed, but on subsequent appeal to the Supreme Court of the United States it was reversed. During this incarceration in the defense of a principle upon which, in his opinion, the very existence of The Mercantile Agency depended, Mr. Douglass was visited by all of the employees in the New York office and presented with the Address reproduced on the opposite page. He subsequently stated that his determined refusal to answer the question put to him "aided greatly in establishing the agencies in the confidence of the public,

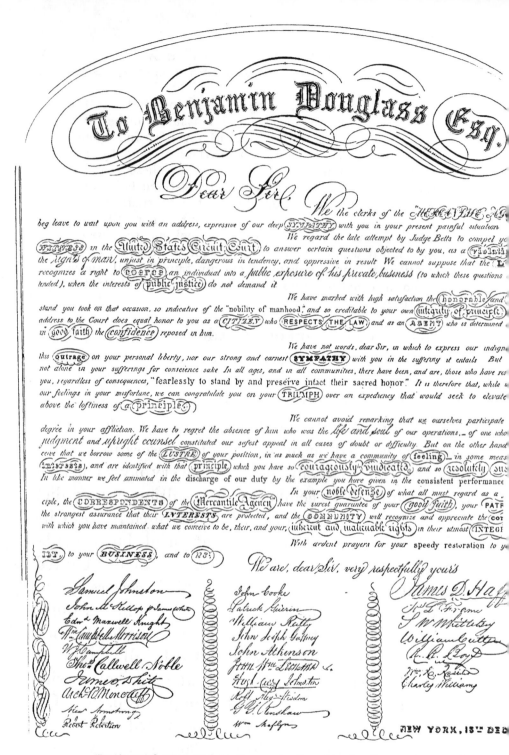

Testimonial presented to Benjamin Douglass by the employees of
The Mercantile Agency, December 15th, 1851

because men saw that they could give information to the agencies, and that these would not betray the confidence reposed in them."* His action in this matter was so highly regarded by his fellow citizens that a delegation of them, headed by Horace Greeley, waited upon him to offer the nomination to the office of Mayor of the city. This offer he was compelled to decline, because the cares and responsibilities of the management of the Agency were such that he did not feel at liberty, in justice to his associates and subscribers, to relinquish them for the sake of seeking political preferment. Later opinion has confirmed the judgment of his contemporaries with respect to the merits of the position taken by Mr. Douglass and the courage with which he maintained his convictions. "In its way, his action was like that of John Hampden." "His refusal to answer a question tending to disclose matters communicated to him in confidence . . . shows a high degree of honor and courage, and his statement of his reasons is lofty and noble in expression." "He was as true as steel." These are some typical comments.

In 1852 the chain of offices operated by The Mercantile Agency was further extended by a branch at Pittsburgh. The Philadelphia office had already obtained a number of subscribers among the leading firms there, but in accordance with his policy of having no more semi-independent branches Mr.

---

*Joseph W. Errant, *The Law Relating to Mercantile Agencies,* page 22. Mr. Errant adds: "The judgment for the plaintiff in this case is, of course, an exception, and must be attributed to the fact that the courts and the public were not yet educated up to the needs and objects of the mercantile agencies."

Douglass opened the Pittsburgh office under the firm style of B. Douglass & Co. The Philadelphia office wrote up a set of books for the younger office to start with, comprising the names on its records for Western Pennsylvania, Western Maryland, Southwestern Virginia, and Southern and Eastern Ohio. At that time Pittsburgh had 46,601 inhabitants and was already one of the foremost industrial centers in the country. In 1853 an office was established at Charleston, South Carolina, under the firm style of B. Douglass & Co. In those days the South was relatively much more developed than the North and West, cotton being a staple

Pittsburgh Office, opened 1852
The present office occupies the entire 11th
floor of the Keenan Building

that was in steady demand for export. Charleston had a population of 42,985 in the census of 1850, as compared with 29,963 for Chicago at the same date. The fact that Mr. Douglass had for a time engaged in business there may have also influenced his decision to make this the tenth office in the Agency chain. The rapid growth of the Agency during this period is indicated by the fact that in 1854 the number of subscribers of the Philadelphia office reached 1,000, Mr. Goodrich giving a dinner at the Merchants' Hotel, in honor of the event.

On June 1st of that year Benjamin Douglass assumed the sole ownership of The Mercantile Agency. As this date marks so important a change in the control of the institution it may also be taken as terminating the period during which the policies were in process of development. As we have seen, Benjamin Douglass was the dominant factor in shaping the destinies of the Agency during this period of its history and the fact that it has survived to this day was undoubtedly due to his efforts. He had during these few years greatly strengthened the chain of branch offices in the South and West, compelled every office to report traders in its district for the benefit of all, and, by his unswerving fidelity to principle in the Beardsley trial, established the fact that information given to the Agency in confidence would be forever held inviolable.

CHAPTER III

The Agency Becomes a National Institution

1854–1859

On assuming the sole ownership of The Mercantile Agency, Mr. Douglass made Robert Graham Dun a partner, the firm style at New York becoming B. Douglass & Co., while at Boston, Philadelphia, Baltimore and Cincinnati the branches continued under the same names as before. Five of the other branches were now trading under the name of B. Douglass & Co., St. Louis and Louisville having changed to that style prior to 1854. In an advertising circular written in 1854, after recounting the list of branch offices already organized, the author gives a most interesting account of the activities of the Agency at that date:

> In all these places, as well as in New York, The Mercantile Agency is liberally patronized by the banks and bankers, as well as merchants of every description.
>
> The troubles of 1837 made the necessity for its existence apparent. The requirements of trade, the general accuracy of the information, and the great good which it was found to accomplish, gave it general favor and acceptance, and, for the last seven or eight years, the onward progress of the Agency has been very rapid. It now employs in the New York office some sixty-five clerks, most of whom are constantly engaged in recording the information daily received and in attending upon the numerous calls of its subscribers.

Every merchant, banker, lawyer and trader, great or small, is, in the sphere of his own operations, a mercantile agency. This institution does on a large scale what individuals have done on a small one. Merchants, by uniting in its support, obtain better information, and on much more reasonable terms, than they could otherwise procure at any expense which could be afforded. About one hundred and twenty-five thousand dollars is yearly expended in this business and the amount of this expense is necessarily increasing. The proprietors have determined to be up to the times and to afford all the assistance and encouragement to the legitimate trade of the country which their means and extensive ramifications will allow them to do.

The first Broadway office of The Mercantile Agency—B. Douglass & Co.—was located on the first floor of the old Trinity Building, 111 Broadway, shown at the left, from 1854 to 1857

As an evidence of their determination "to be up to the times," the firm proceeded vigorously to extend their chain of offices in the West and South. In 1854, the very year of the new partnership, a branch office was opened at Chicago. That city was then just beginning to assume the aspect of a commercial metropolis, though on a small scale as measured by present standards. In 1823 the village consisted of ten or twelve houses and 60 or 70 inhabitants. In 1832 there were five small stores and 250 inhabitants. In 1840 it contained four foreign commission houses, 97 retail stores, 11 lumber yards, one furnace, two flour mills, one distillery, three printing offices, one bindery, two daily and two weekly newspapers. The population was 4,470. At that date the first railroad had not yet reached what was destined to become the greatest railroad center in the world. All merchandise arrived and departed by lake vessels and by the Illinois & Michigan Canal, which connected the little lake port with the head of

Chicago Office, established 1854
Present quarters, entire 13th and part of
12th floors, New York Life Building

steamboat navigation on the Illinois River, through which, in turn, it reached all parts of the Mississippi River Valley. Ten years later the population had increased to 29,963 (Census of 1850), and by 1854 had quite likely risen to double that total, for then the railroads had come at last and the era of Chicago's astounding commercial expansion had dawned. The early date at which this office was established is of interest as illustrating the keenness with which the chiefs of the Agency foresaw the trend of commercial growth.

In 1856 offices were established at Detroit and at Richmond, Va., the latter under the style of Pratt & Co., as a branch of J. D. Pratt & Co., of Baltimore. It was the last office to be established under a style entirely different from that of the parent organization. The Chicago and Detroit offices were organized under the firm style of B. Douglass & Co. In April, 1855,

Detroit Office, established 1856
The present quarters occupy 3,147 square feet in Union Trust Company Building

Mr. Douglass bought out Mr. Goodrich at Philadelphia and changed the style there to B. Douglass & Co. The following year an office was opened at Dubuque, Iowa—the fourteenth in the Agency chain.

Thus far, the growth of The Mercantile Agency had been confined within the limits of the United

States. The year 1857 was a notable one in the annals of the organization as marking its first extension into foreign lands, branch offices being established at London, England, and Montreal, Canada. The London office was opened September 1st, under the style of B. Douglass & Co. One of the first steps taken by the manager of the new branch to acquaint the mercantile community with the nature and purposes of the institution was to issue a London edition of the circular quoted on pages 55-56, together with a reprint of the article in *Hunt's Merchants' Magazine* of January, 1851. The printing was done by Jones & Causton, Eastcheap and Pudding Lane,

Richmond Office, established 1856
At present located in Mutual Building, close to the hub of Richmond's activities

and the little circular is a beautiful example of the printer's art.

There was a need for such literature, for the mercantile agency idea, as it had been originated and developed in the United States by Messrs. Tappan and Douglass and their associates in The Mercantile

Agency, was then new to the United Kingdom. The London office was opened primarily because the New York office already had on its ledgers as clients the names of a number of the leading export houses in the United Kingdom. The interests of these clients could be better served by an office in their own country, while such a branch enabled the Agency to offer the facilities of its organization to houses in the United States which required the protection thus afforded for the safe conduct of commercial transactions across the Atlantic. This first outpost in the Agency's now world-wide chain of offices overseas was originally located in a small room in the Unity Building, 10 Cannon

London Office, established 1857
The first branch of the Agency abroad—
now at Kings' House, King St., Cheapside

Street, London, E. C., but the business proved so successful that six years later larger quarters were secured at 24 Basinghall Street. At the outset, the London branch confined its business to export and import houses trading between the two countries, but it was not long before the mercantile

60

community in Great Britain began to perceive the value of the service, and the office found itself called upon to report to clients on British as well as American traders. At present, and for many years past, this has constituted by far the larger part of the business of the London branch, necessitating the establishment of suboffices at Glasgow, Scotland, in 1872, and, more recently, at Manchester and Birmingham, England, and at Belfast, Ireland. It is an interesting

Montreal Office, established 1857
Now occupying most of the third floor of the east wing in the
Board of Trade Building

fact that "Subscriber No. 1" of the London office, a prominent house, has been continuously on its books since 1857.

The first branch of The Mercantile Agency in Canada was established at Montreal the same year as that at London. Its purpose was for a time misunderstood by the conservative business community of the colony, which did not see that the institution was designed to meet their own needs. This made it

difficult at the outset to glean the information necessary for the compilation of mercantile reports.   The

The office of B. Douglass & Co. at 314 Broadway in 1858
This was the head office of The Mercantile Agency from 1857 to 1864
and again from 1878 until 1898

ability and tact of the early managers gradually
overcame this difficulty, however, and the rapid

growth of the business in later years affords ample evidence of the general confidence and esteem with which the Agency is now regarded throughout that country, where at present it operates offices in nearly every important mercantile center from the Atlantic to the Pacific. During the year 1858 the list of offices was further extended by the opening of branches at Cleveland, Ohio; Milwaukee, Wis.; and Toronto, Canada.

An interesting contemporary picture of the activities of The Mercantile Agency at this period of its development has been preserved for us in the pages of the *Bankers' Magazine and Statistical Register,* of New York. In its issue for January, 1858, this periodical devoted several pages to an account of the system as it then existed. The following extracts from this description of the Agency as it appeared to an observer fifty-eight years ago are still of interest:

THE MERCANTILE AGENCY SYSTEM

I.—ITS FIRST ORGANIZATION.   II.—ITS IMMEDIATE OBJECTS.
III.—ITS COLLATERAL BENEFITS.

The Mercantile Agency is the name used by a firm having its headquarters in New York, and branch houses in the leading cities of the United States; and in Montreal, Canada, and London, England. The principal object of the Agency is to supply to annual subscribers information respecting the character, capacity and pecuniary condition of persons asking credit. The valuable services it has rendered to the domestic trade of the country, as a check upon our credit system, are acknowledged by the mercantile community. Its history, together with an explanation of its mode of operation, may not be without interest to the general reader and foreign merchant.

The Agency was first established in 1841, in the city of New York, by Mr. Lewis Tappan, and was conducted by him, upon a comparatively limited scale, until 1846, when Mr. Benjamin Douglass became his co-adjutor, and assumed the chief management. From this time the business increased rapidly, and assumed a permanent and recognized position among the mercantile institutions of the country. In 1849, Mr. Lewis Tappan disposed of his entire interest in the business to Mr. Douglass and Mr. Arthur Tappan, who formed a partnership to continue five years, at the end of which time, and by virtue of agreements prospectively entered into, Mr. Douglass became sole proprietor; and the present style was adopted with the admission of Mr. R. Graham Dun.

Our limits will not permit us to trace, step by step, the growth of the Agency, or to dwell upon the personal aspects of its history. Founded upon the interests of merchants, and conducted from the beginning by men of ability, capacity for work, high character, and thorough knowledge of the wants of mercantile business, its progress has been uninterrupted. From New York it has extended its branch and associate offices to seventeen other cities, viz., Philadelphia, Boston, Montreal, Baltimore, Richmond, Petersburg, Charleston, New Orleans, Pittsburgh, Cleveland, Cincinnati, Chicago, Milwaukee, Dubuque, St. Louis, Detroit, and London, England. All these branches are under the direction of the proprietors at New York, and are governed by uniform rules. A daily interchange of information facilitates the answering of the inquiries of the respective subscribers for all parts of the country.

It is obvious that the gigantic labor of reporting the business men of Canada and the United States could not be performed by any one office, nor could the expense be borne by the merchants of any one city. B. Douglass & Co. perform it by means of their system of branch offices, each supported by the subscriptions of the merchants, bankers and manufacturers of the city in which it is located. The district allotted to

An interior view of the main office of Dun, Boyd & Co., The Mercantile Agency, at 314-316 Broadway, as it appeared from 1857 to 1864. When re-occupied in 1878 the main entrance was removed to the front of the building—as here shown it was at the rear

65

each office is the section of the country of which the city in which it is located is the trade center. For instance, the Boston office reports that portion of the New England States of which it has the chief trade; the Dubuque, the great part of Iowa; the Milwaukee, Wisconsin; the Charleston, South Carolina and Georgia; while the Ohio Valley is divided between the offices at Pittsburgh, Cincinnati and Louisville.

This subdivision of labor is the means of securing a minuteness and accuracy of reports, which, to any one unacquainted with the machinery of the Agency, is truly astonishing. The operations of a branch office do not embrace a large extent of country. They are usually limited to the 150 or 200 counties, the majority of whose traders buy their goods chiefly at the city where it is established. In each of these counties the principal of the office secures one, two, three, or more correspondents, the number varying with the population and the division of the local trade among the towns. These correspondents are selected for their integrity, long residence in the county, general acquaintance, business experience and judgment. Their duties are to advise the Agency promptly, by letter or telegraph, of every change affecting the standing or responsibility of traders; to notify it of suits, protests, mortgages, losses by fire, endorsements or otherwise; to answer all special inquiries addressed to them by any of the associate offices; and to revise before each trade season, or oftener if required, the previous reports of every trader in the county, noting any change for the better or worse. No report is considered full unless it embraces, in regard to each trader, his business, the length of time he has pursued it, his success, or the contrary, his age, character, habits, capacity, means, prospects, property out of business, real estate, judgments, mortgages or other liens upon his property. The greatest care is taken in selecting the agents, who furnish the bulk of the information to the Agency. Their integrity of character, freedom from prejudice, and from any entangling connections with mercantile men which might bias them in their reports, their social position, influence and opportunities for knowing thoroughly the men they are reporting, are all taken carefully into consideration, and the very great success and expansion of the business is, we have little doubt, to be attributed, in a great measure, to the judgment and careful discrimination which has been exercised in this particular. Nevertheless, after all this care in the selection of the agents, prudence would seem to require some check upon them. This is done by traveling agents who are sent through the country, and who report the traders upon their own resources, and generally without any knowledge of what the local agent has previously reported. Their reports are compared carefully with those of the local agent, and any discrepancy thoroughly investigated. Again, much information of a most valuable character is derived from special correspondents, as bank cashiers, insurance agents, notaries public, sheriffs, and others, whose official position gives them peculiar opportunities of knowing not only the resources and character of business men, but also the degree of promptness with which they meet their business obligations. Another source of information is that afforded by merchants themselves, who frequently make "statements" of their own affairs from their books. These are given under their own signature, with the avowed purpose of having them used by the Agency as a basis for credit. The leading facts contained in such "statements" are, of course, always made a matter of special investigation. For instance, a merchant in his "statement" says he owns a farm or a number of town lots, in a certain county, worth a certain sum. The records of the county are examined to see if any such property stands in his name; the estimate he puts upon it is compared with that given by persons acquainted with the value of property in that locality; and, lastly, a careful examination is made to ascertain if any encumbrance exists against it, not mentioned in the voluntary statement of the merchant. All the other facts in his statement are scrutinized in like manner, and it is thus subjected to a very searching analysis. Reports obtained with the care thus exhibited and from such a variety of sources, must certainly approach as near perfection as is practicable under any circumstances.

The records of each office are arranged according to counties. Each partnership and individual name is indexed for convenience of reference on inquiry being made by subscribers. The reports coming in daily are copied without delay in the book for the county to which they refer, and transmitted by mail or express to the next or central office. All unfavorable information is promptly copied on slips, and sent simultaneously to all the offices whose subscribers' interests are probably involved therein. Serious embarrassments, assignments and failures are telegraphed. The mass of information thus contributed by the branches to the central office passes into the hands of the chief clerk, is distributed by him to the heads of departments, by them in their turn parceled out among the clerks, and by these last recorded and indexed in the proper books. The records of the New York office of The Mercantile Agency contain the aggregate knowledge of traders possessed by the seventeen most flourishing mercantile communities in North America. . . .

A comparison of the system of The Mercantile Agency with that of the "Commercial Traveler," which it superseded, is much to the advantage of the former, as regards the item of cost as well as information. From a large dry goods house we learn that, in old times, its expenses for travelers counted by thousands, and that it was, to a vexatious extent, in the power of clerks, who were anxious to make sales, and whose good opinion was more often won by civilities than by responsibility. Now, it holds an efficient check upon its salesmen, who travel, not to choose customers, but to make collections, and obtain orders from those chosen by the firm.

We need not multiply illustrations. The usefulness of the Agency is unquestionable. Without it, the credit system, in a country like ours, with vast distances between seller and buyer, would make mercantile pursuits the most uncertain of all. Its principal advantages are as follows:

It points out to the city merchant solvent, prudent and thriving customers; cautions him against the doubtful; and apprizes him promptly of changes which make it proper to press the collection of his claims.

It makes the solvent and punctual trader known in every city giving him credit, and dispenses altogether with letters of introduction or guarantees.

It protects him from the ruinous competition of the inexperienced, the incompetent and the fraudulent.

It prevents delay in the delivery of goods ordered, giving full reports of the purchaser.

It corrects many evils incident to the credit system, and tends to keep commercial business in the hands of men of integrity, means and experience.

It tends to promote a high standard of mercantile honor, to check speculation and extravagance, to enhance the value of punctuality and good character, and to make it the interest of every trader to be temperate, industrious, economical and desirous of an unspotted reputation.

Future changes in the credit system of the United States may introduce new features into the Agency, and modify its machinery; but the experience and thorough business ability of the present proprietors are sufficient guarantee that all modifications will be in accordance with the wants of the mercantile community.

This picture of the activities of The Mercantile Agency of fifty-eight years ago is of interest as showing the care and thoroughness with which it collected the valuable information it was designed to supply. Later years have brought many changes and improvements, but the success of the institution is largely due to the work of its original founders—to the sound principles of credit investigation laid down by Lewis Tappan, and to the genius for systematization and organization displayed by Benjamin Douglass in expanding and co-ordinating the work of the various branches.

In 1857 The Mercantile Agency began the publication of detailed statistics regarding mercantile failures in the United States and Canada. It was immediately recognized as the national authority on this subject—a fact that justifies the title selected for this chapter. As the first report issued presented the failures for the year 1856, the returns compiled and published by The Mercantile Agency now cover a period of six decades, during two of which they were the only statistics on the subject.

It is difficult to ascertain after a lapse of sixty years precisely when and how the idea of compiling and publishing failure statistics for the country as a whole originated. Probably, however, like most conceptions of real and lasting value, it was a matter of gradual development. At all events, certain facts are matters of record, and these, when set down in their chronological order, give a fairly clear and complete history of the inception and early development of this phase of The Mercantile Agency's work. On January 17th, 1856, the New York *Independent* published the following paragraphs on the subject of credit in its column headed "Commercial and Financial":

> The time has come when a more rigid credit system must be adopted, not only in New York, but all over the country. Probably nine-tenths of the failures which have ever occurred in large cities can be directly traced either to recklessness or bad management in giving credits. Many a concern has started with fair prospects for a prosperous career, but, determining to distinguish themselves at the outset, have plunged headlong the first year into a long credit business amounting to more than

twenty times the capital invested. We mean literally what we say. The mistake once made can seldom ever be remedied. The concern is crippled, and its brilliant prospects fade away. . . .

We commend the whole subject of credits to the consideration of our mercantile readers, and urge them to take such action as will fairly inaugurate a reform, indispensable to their prosperity and healthful in its influence upon the country.

Do you doubt the importance of this subject? Then look over the balance sheet just completed, and see if what we say is not important. Look at your interest account, and you will doubtless obtain some light from that quarter. Look over your bad debts, and by that time you will probably be satisfied. Probe matters to the bottom, and see if carelessness and recklessness in giving credits have not done you more damage than all other influences combined. If you are convinced of the fact, change your course in future, or never open your mouth with murmurings if your career is speedily run, and you fall into the ranks of the Broken Merchants' Army.

Nothing was said in the passages just quoted about inaugurating a new department in the journal, and a new departure in the annals of business, but the following week (January 24th, 1856) in the same "Commercial and Financial" section, there appeared a brief summary of a contemporary failure, which was followed by similar items each week until the feature began to attract national attention. This interesting and valuable information was obtained from The Mercantile Agency, and was thus the forerunner of the Agency's systematic compilation of failure returns. In *Hunt's Merchants' Magazine* for February, 1857 (vol. xxxvi, p. 595), appeared a brief summary of the failures for 1856, by States, as follows:

MERCANTILE FAILURES IN 1856

The following statement of failures in the United States during the year 1856, emanated from "The Mercantile Agency" of the city of New York:

MERCANTILE FAILURES IN THE UNITED STATES FOR THE YEAR 1856.

STATES:	Failures.	Swindling failures.	In a precarious condition.	STATES:	Failures.	Swindling failures.	In a precarious condition.
New York	708	31	119	New Jersey	35	..	21
Ohio	241	10	13	Missouri	32	2	6
Pennsylvania	234	7	6	Vermont	32	1	16
Massachusetts	179	7	6	South Carolina	31	2	3
Illinois	169	15	4	Tennessee	28	1	6
Virginia	146	6	31	Louisiana	24	4	5
Michigan	92	6	23	New Hampshire	23	..	..
Wisconsin	81	6	14	Rhode Island	22	..	3
Maine	68	10	10	Minnesota	21	..	10
British Provinces	67	6	18	Alabama	18	2	2
Iowa	57	7	5	Territories & California	17	3	7
Connecticut	53	..	14				
North Carolina	53	5	31	Texas	16	..	4
Georgia	47	3	10	Florida	12	..	..
Maryland and Delaware	44	5	8	Arkansas	8	..	..
Kentucky	38	..	4	Total	2,705		

The weekly reports of failures, published originally in the *Independent,* are made up at The Mercantile Agency, and we have no doubt are correct. The facilities which that institution has at command keep it well posted. The failures reported last year (1856) amount to more than twenty-seven hundred in number, and it would not be extravagant to put them down at an average of $20,000 each, which would give an aggregate of $54,100,000. The probability is that the creditors of these failures have not received, on an average, more than 25 per cent. of their claims, which involves a loss of $40,000,000.

This is the first return of failures for the whole of the United States and Canada ever published, and was the starting point of the series of reports on this important subject that have since been compiled and issued by The Mercantile Agency without interruption. The intimate connection between mercantile failures and the general condition of trade and industry during the period when the bankruptcies took place led naturally, and almost inevitably, to the preparation of a review of the business situation in conjunction with the statistics showing the commercial mortality. The circular of January, 1858, issued by B. Douglass & Co., The Mercantile Agency, gave an extensive and interesting review of the panic of 1857, together with a table showing the "Statistics as to Failures from December 25th, 1856, to December 25th, 1857." This

Cleveland Office, established 1858
At present occupying 6,000 square feet of floor space in the Century Building

table reported 5,123 failures, as against 2,705 for the year 1856, and also gave the returns for some of the large cities, as well as for each of the States and Canada. Both the number of failures and liabilities were given in each case. The circular for January, 1859, omitted these subdivisions, but gave comparative figures for the preceding year. The circular issued in January, 1860, contained a veritable broadside of statistics, giving all of the subdivisions of two years before and comparative statistics for 1857, in addition to those for 1859. The annual circulars for the next few years were less elaborate, giving only the number of failures and amount of liabilities for the Northern States and Canada— no figures regarding the South being available. Fortunately, the record by States was kept up, with the exception of one or two years, and these omissions were supplied by the comparative tables of later years. The circular of January, 1863, for example, gave the returns of failures by States for each year from 1857 to 1862. In each of these circulars the failure statistics were supplemented by brief reviews of business con-

Milwaukee Office, established 1858
This office occupies most of western half of the third floor in the Wells Building

ditions—reviews all the more valuable to the student of the mercantile history of the period because they were contemporary analyses made by men more than ordinarily familiar with the situation.

About 1869 the annual circulars took on a more uniform style, the table being placed on the first page, and from one to three previous years being included for purposes of comparison—the compilers realizing that statistics covering a single year would be useless. On April 23rd, 1875, The Mercantile Agency began the publication of quarterly failure returns, prefacing its

Toronto Office, established 1858
Occupying about 4,000 square feet of floor space in Dominion Bank Building

table for the first three months of 1875 with these words:

> The very general interest displayed by the public in the "Statistics of Failures," which we have hitherto presented at the end of the year in our Annual Circular, has induced us to devote special attention to the compila-

tion of these figures, and, at the request of prominent commercial authorities, we will hereafter publish the returns at the conclusion of each quarter of the year.

The semi-annual returns for that year included a detailed review of the business outlook, as did the report covering failures for the three-quarter period. This practice has since been continued, and in 1884 detailed reports regarding business conditions from each of the branch offices in the United States and Canada were included with the circular covering failures for the first six months of each year. On August 5th, 1893, DUN'S REVIEW was started, and these reports of business conditions were made a weekly feature, while failures were reported weekly and monthly as well as by quarters and annually. In these statistics names and individual amounts are never given.

Through the leading press associations these failure statistics and the weekly summary of business conditions throughout the country, as reported in DUN'S REVIEW, are now telegraphed to more than 2,400 daily newspapers for their Saturday morning editions. Altogether, including papers supplied direct from the office of DUN'S REVIEW, upwards of 2,670 publications in the United States and Canada are now receiving the figures regularly. At times when business conditions in the United States are deemed to be critical, these reviews of the situation and failure statistics are frequently cabled to all of the leading European capitals.

CHAPTER IV

The Development of The Mercantile Agency's Reference Book

1859–1870

ON May 1st, 1859, Benjamin Douglass sold his entire interest in The Mercantile Agency to his partner, Robert G. Dun, and retired from the business to the upbuilding and development of which he had devoted all of his energies for thirteen years. But for the work of Mr. Douglass during this critical and formative period of its history, it is altogether probable that the institution founded by Lewis Tappan in 1841 would not have survived the fifties, if, indeed, it had lived to enter that stormy decade. A credit reporting agency that did not cover the South as well as the North and West would have been of very limited value to merchants, for the South was then the nation's great buying region. Mr. Douglass gave the Agency its foremost position in the South. He also kept it in the vanguard with the pioneers who were then pushing across the great central plain and out into the West. He expanded The Mercantile Agency from an institution having only four small offices on the Eastern seaboard into a nation-wide organization, with a well developed extension in Canada and a suc-

cessful outpost in Europe. Of the nineteen offices in operation in the year 1859, sixteen were
in the United States, two in Canada and one at
London, England. In the five years from 1854 to 1859
alone the business had more than doubled, while the inauguration of its annual compilation of failure statistics gave the Agency the prestige of being a national authority on a subject of vital interest to the
business community. More important still, by his unswerving loyalty to principle in the trial of 1851, Mr.
Douglass had won the confidence and respect of the
country and established the fact, once for all, that
the Agency could be implicitly relied upon to keep
inviolate the source of information given to it in confidence.

Mr. Dun, who now became the sole proprietor of
The Mercantile Agency, was at that time not quite
thirty-three years old. He possessed in a very high
degree the gift—much more valuable than genius—of
being able to surround himself with men of ability.
Instead of attempting, like his predecessors, to direct
the policies of the institution single-handed, he at
once organized an executive administration consisting
of four men—Charles Barlow, Robert B. Boyd, Matthias B. Smith, and himself. Under that organization
the four associates, to all the world except themselves,
were partners—each having all the powers and liabilities of a partner—but, between themselves, three of
them were without the rights of partners. Mr. Dun
continued to be the sole owner of everything connected

with the business which could be the subject of ownership, and for the services of the other three he paid

From a painting by Benjamin Constant
ROBERT GRAHAM DUN
Sole proprietor of The Mercantile Agency of R. G. DUN & CO.
from 1859 to 1900—a period of forty-one years

sums of money which were measured by a percentage
of the profits.   That plan Mr. Dun followed until his

death. The partners changed from time to time, but as the nature of their relation to him always remained the same, the business was protected from the disruptive effects which might follow the dissolution of a partnership in which the members had proprietary rights.

The great event of the year in which the change in ownership just described took place was the publication of The Mercantile Agency's first Reference Book. This was issued February 1st, 1859, or three months before Mr. Douglass relinquished his ownership. Mr. Douglass was strongly opposed to the idea of a reference book as a key or indication as to the nature of the Agency's reports by means of ratings. He maintained that the sole business of The Mercantile Agency should be to compile and issue reports, and that a book of ratings would only be misleading and tend to create trouble and dissatisfaction. The fact that the first book was published while he was still proprietor, however, would seem to indicate that he had either changed his views, or had agreed to allow his successor to begin the task soon after the change in ownership was agreed upon, and long before it was carried into effect.

The first Reference Book was a quaint, old-fashioned affair compared with those issued at present. It was bound in dark brown sheepskin covers (nearly red) extra strong and thick, and with a lock, so that the proprietor of the subscribing firm might retain a key and thus keep its precious contents from the prying eyes of his subordinates or visitors. The volume contained 519 pages, 10⅝ inches high by 8¾ wide,

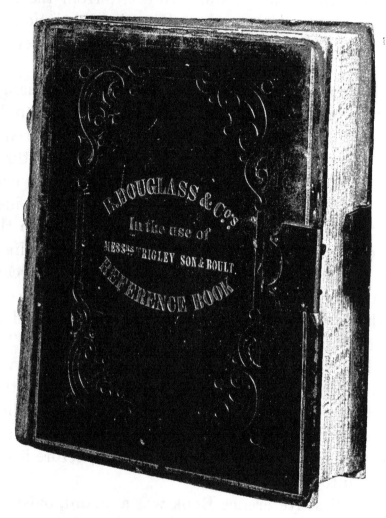

*The first Reference Book issued by B. Douglass & Co., The
Mercantile Agency, in 1859—showing the curious lock
to keep its contents from prying eyes*

with a maximum of 42 names to a page; an index to cities and towns of two pages, and one of firm names, arranged alphabetically, of 43 pages. The title-page read as follows:

THE

MERCANTILE AGENCY'S

REFERENCE BOOK,

OF THE

UNITED STATES AND BRITISH PROVINCES:

CONTAINING RATINGS

OF THE

PRINCIPAL WHOLESALE MERCHANTS (TOGETHER WITH SOME RETAILERS) AND MANUFACTURERS.

FOR THE YEAR

1859.

NEW YORK:
B. DOUGLASS AND COMPANY, 314 BROADWAY.
1859.

Title-page of the first Reference Book
An exact reproduction a little over one-third actual size

No less than four different ratings for each firm were given: B. Douglass & Co.'s ratings (1) for Bankers and Buyers of single-name paper; (2) for

Commission Merchants; and (3) for Importers, Manufacturers and Jobbers; and, lastly, a Summary of Merchants' and Bankers' ratings. The top of a typical page is reproduced herewith showing these ratings, or "markings," as they are called in the preface.

466   ILLINOIS.

	NAME.	BUSINESS.	LOCATION.	For Bankers & Buyers of single-name paper.	For Com. Merchants.	For Importers, Manufacturers, & Jobbers.	An Outside Marking.
					B. D. & Co.'s Markings.		
1	Fuller, Smith & Bishop,	*Grocers.*	Galena.		1+	2	2
2	Fricke, Herman,	*Jeweller.*	do.		3	2½	3
3	Felt, Benj. F.	*Grocer.*	do.	3	2½	2	2
4	Ferguson, Geo.,	*General Store.*	do.	3	2½	2	2
5	Grant, S. S.,	*Leather.*	do.	3	2+	2	2

Top of a page in the 1859 Reference Book, the last line referring to the tannery conducted by Ulysses S. Grant, afterward President of the United States, under the name of his father

In the front of the volume was pasted the

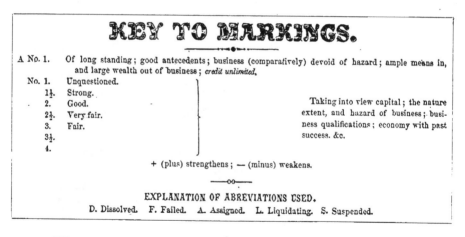

KEY TO MARKINGS.

A No. 1.   Of long standing; good antecedents; business (comparatively) devoid of hazard; ample means in, and large wealth out of business; *credit unlimited.*

No. 1.   Unquestioned.
1½.   Strong.
2.   Good.
2½.   Very fair.
3.   Fair.
3½.
4.

Taking into view capital; the nature extent, and hazard of business; business qualifications; economy with past success. &c.

+ (plus) strengthens; — (minus) weakens.

EXPLANATION OF ABBREVIATIONS USED.
D. Dissolved.   F. Failed.   A. Assigned.   L. Liquidating.   S. Suspended.

The reason for presenting four distinct, and occasionally contradictory, ratings is explained at some length in the preface, as follows:

PREFACE

We have prepared this work for certain classes of
our employers whose business interests have long demanded it. The labor and responsibility connected with
its faithful and impartial performance have hitherto
deterred us from the undertaking. Persuaded, however,
that aside from the obligation we owed our employers,
to promote and protect their interests in this our spe-
cialty, we should be greatly increasing the facilities for
transacting business, and conferring a benefit on the
community, we were led the more cheerfully to assume
the labor it involved.

Above the retailer there are five classes of business
men conducting the commerce of the world. Profit
determines the risks taken; hence the standard of one is
not that of the other: a single classification, therefore,
would not suit the wants of all. We have found three
ratings necessary: one for Bankers, one for Commission
Merchants, and a third for the common benefit of
Importers, Manufacturers and Jobbers.

The Banker loans his money on interest. Having no
other consideration, it should be a fundamental principle
with him, in all cases to be secure. His judgment should
be rigid. The Commission Merchant, however, has
other inducements than that of interest on his capital—
he has two commissions. His guarantee charge creates
a fund out of which to meet losses, not, however, sufficient to justify much hazard; for which reason his
judgment should be highly conservative. But with the
Importer, Manufacturer and Jobber, under the stimulus
of good profits, a larger liberality is expected. Holding these views, we have adapted our markings
accordingly.

We have made them from a contemplation of all the
circumstances pertaining to each case. They are based
upon the historical facts upon our records, often running
back eighteen years, regarding the business training,
the moral and business fitness, the capital, the nature,
extent and hazards of business, &c.; we have, moreover, searched the records as to the condition of the real
estate of many parties. In the absence of knowledge of
this kind, there can be no *accurate* marking.

In order to comprehend fully our views as to the comparative merits of houses, the three markings should be read in conjunction. They should act and re-act upon one another. To those who have a right to consult us as to the details upon which our ratings are founded, we shall be happy at all times to show cause for our markings, where they differ from the opinion generally entertained.

B. DOUGLASS & Co.

The 1859 Reference Book contained altogether 20,268 names, apportioned among the various States and the Canadian Provinces as follows:

Massachusetts	2,475	South Carolina	506
Maine	201	Georgia	348
New Hampshire	38	Alabama	221
Rhode Island	726	Tennessee	156
Vermont	16	Louisiana	690
Connecticut	437	Michigan	200
New York	6,340	Illinois	375
Ohio	1,334	Wisconsin	72
Pennsylvania	1,550	Iowa	227
New Jersey	187	Minnesota	75
Delaware	18	Nova Scotia	168
Maryland	840	New Brunswick	62
Virginia	585	Newfoundland	79
Kentucky	336	Prince Edward Island	56
Missouri	520	Canada East	551
North Carolina	40	Canada West	839

One perfect copy of the 1859 Reference Book, with all the "points," as the book collectors say, is still in the possession of the Agency. It was originally issued to Wrigley Sons & Boult, and has their name embossed on the front cover. The archives also contain the copy used by the Louisville office. It shows evidence of hard use. The preface, list of cities, and last page are gone, but on a series of blank pages interleaved between those of the book itself are some of the oldest reports that have come down to us in their original form. Human documents, they are, these Southern pen pictures of the olden time—not dry-as-dust records. Here is one that must have been written by some Southern gentleman of the old school, possibly a clerk of court or County Judge. It is regarding a party in Monroe County, Georgia. Note the quaint abbreviations to save time and ink:

———— ———— Groc. & Confect.
Will phps. enlarge his bus. Owns but little ppy. Is sol. steady & attent. to his bus. Considd hon. & relia. His bus. has been done on a vy sml scale, so much so as not to be kn. outsd of the village in wh. he resides. If Cr. is given him the reliance must be upon his honor to pay—and I kn. of 00 / to impeach it.

From a circular bearing the date of December 20th, 1859, it appears that the second volume of the Reference Book was issued in installments between January 1st and February 1st, 1860. The circular states:

We have now 17 branch offices, and when you consider the great advantage we possess through constant intercourse, by telegraph and otherwise, and that this extended information furnished you is constantly watched and revised and that you are daily notified of all changes that come under our observation, we trust you will appreciate both it and our efforts.

The first part of the volume, embracing all interests connected with the Foreign and Home Commerce and the Produce of the United States and British North America, will be issued on the 1st of January, 1860. The first edition will be necessarily limited, inasmuch as the press will be employed to bring out the other parts of the volume in due season. If you desire a copy of

this first edition, by early application at the office it can
be secured.

This part will be immediately followed by the other
interests, classified and sub-divided, and also the entire
volume, uniting the whole and embracing the principal
merchants and corporate and manufacturing companies
in the United States and British North America.

The preface to the second volume refers briefly
to the favor with which the first had been received:

The unexampled appreciation of our former issue,
together with the solicitation of friends, has induced us
to publish a new, enlarged, and very much more complete edition, embracing, with the exception of the
Pacific Coast, the entire Union and British North
America.

Each specific trade, together with all such branches
as perfectly harmonize in interest, form separate Parts.
These Parts we offer separately, or collectively, as may
be desired. This has been especially solicited to enable
the merchant to possess himself, at moderate cost, of
that in which he has a direct interest. For the convenience of bankers and others, we combine the different Parts, forming one whole volume.

It also announced one important change in the
list of ratings reported:

In our last we were induced to give the popular
trade-markings. These, in very many cases, were dis-
crepant, and many of our subscribers have mistaken
them for a condensation of our own, thereby creating
confusion. We therefore omit them in this issue. We
have, however, availed ourselves of numerous markings
obtained from the highest authorities, and closely
criticized and examined every case which conflicted with
our own.

In the second volume the publishers attempted
a most elaborate subdivision of traders into six groups
and, as announced in the circular quoted above, issued

the work in six parts, bound separately, or in a general book comprising all six bound together. The archives contain copies of the 1860 book in both forms—even the six separate parts having each its lock. (Five of them, by the way, have been locked for the last fifty-five years, and the keys lost.) The subdivisions introduced into this edition were as follows:

PART   I.--Shipping and Commission, Produce Commission, Groceries, Drugs, Wines and Liquors, Naval Stores, Flour Mills, Ship Chandlers, Distillers, and all other interests that harmonize therewith.

PART   II.—Silk, Cotton and Woolen Goods, Clothing, Carpets, Gentlemen's Furnishings, Laces, Millinery Goods, Upholstery, Umbrellas, and all other interests that harmonize therewith.

PART III.—Boots and Shoes, Findings, Tanners, Hides and Leather, India Rubber Goods, Trunks, Saddle and Harness Makers, &c.

PART   IV.—Hardware, Founders, Metals, House Furnishing Goods, Builders, Carriage, Cabinet and Piano Forte Makers, Planing and Saw Mills, Wooden Ware of all Kinds, Coal, Lumber, Marble, and all interests that harmonize therewith.

PART   V.—Booksellers, Publishers and Stationers, Music Paper Manufacturers, Paper Hangings and Printing Ink, Yankee Notions, Toys and Foreign Fancy Goods, Jewelers, Gold and Silver Manufacturers, Crockery, China, Earthenware, Glass Ware, Plate Glass, and all interests that harmonize therewith.

PART VI.—Hats, Caps, Furs and Straw Goods.

Under the foregoing classifications the book comprised 768 pages, with approximately 30,720 names. In addition to these it contained a list of private bankers, on pages 769 to 785, of 558 names. This plan of subdividing the book into separate lists proved to be impracticable, as many traders could not be clearly classified, even under this elaborate scheme. It was therefore discontinued after the second volume, as the following extract from the preface to the 1861 book shows:

> The favor with which our Reference Book has been received, induces us to continue its publication.
>
> The present edition is not subdivided into classified trades as was our last; nor does it contain the names of that class of small traders a credit to whom can more safely be given by consulting our records. We have adapted the present work to that class of merchants who grant credit as bankers, money-lenders, and wholesale dealers.

The 1861 edition was somewhat smaller than that for 1860, comprising 639 pages and about 25,560 names. In this book the Key to Ratings was changed quite materially, and as the gradual development of this feature of the early Reference Book is a matter of considerable interest to all grantors of credit, the Key is reproduced in full on page 90.

After the publication of the Reference Book for 1861, just described, the Civil War interrupted this important branch of The Mercantile Agency's activities for a period of three years. In 1864, probably in the latter part of the year, the publication of the work was resumed. The earliest edition bears upon its title-page the date 1864-'5 and states that it was

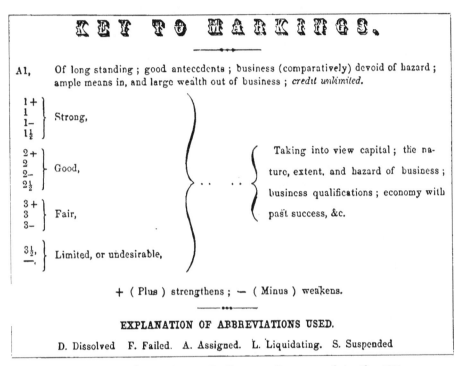

KEY TO MARKINGS.

A1, Of long standing ; good antecedents ; business (comparatively) devoid of hazard ; ample means in, and large wealth out of business ; *credit unlimited.*

1+
1
1−   Strong,
1½

2+
2
2−   Good,   Taking into view capital ; the na-
2½   ture, extent, and hazard of business ;
                    business qualifications ; economy with
3+   past success, &c.
3   Fair,
3−

3½,   Limited, or undesirable,
—.

+ (Plus) strengthens ; — (Minus) weakens.

EXPLANATION OF ABBREVIATIONS USED.

D. Dissolved   F. Failed.   A. Assigned.   L. Liquidating.   S. Suspended

Facsimile of the Key to Ratings as it appeared in the 1861 Reference Book. This Key was a marked improvement over its predecessors

entered for copyright in the year 1864. The following extract from the preface explains the discontinuance of publication caused by the war and the new Key to Ratings, which here appears for the first time:

> The publication of the " Mercantile Agency Reference Book" was discontinued three years ago, in consequence of the unsettled condition of commercial interests incident to civil war. In the sudden and ever-varying changes, affecting all branches of trade, no "ratings" could be made that would be of any permanent value. The detailed reports upon our Records, posted from day

to day, seemed to offer the only reliable aid, and we preferred to rest our reputation upon these, rather than issue a Book of Ratings in which we ourselves could have but little confidence. Latterly, however, business matters having assumed a greater degree of permanence, or a more fixed adaptation to the times, and our subscribers having urged us to a resumption of the work, we have concluded to renew its publication, confidently relying upon the mercantile community for proper appreciation and commensurate support.

The "Key" upon which the ratings are made is entirely our own, and has valuable original features, which we commend to particular observation. It not only shows *what* the mercantile credit of the trader is, but also *why* it is. In other words, it shows how far the conclusions as to mercantile credit are based upon the possession of capital, as well as how far personal and business qualities have been considered in the absence of capital. It must be obvious that this peculiar adaptation of the key affords an excellent opportunity for nice discrimination. It is only through the copious details furnished by our Records that such an idea can be acted upon.

This book contained **33** pages of ratings for New York City and Brooklyn, comprising about **8,000** names; and some **550** pages for the rest of the United States, comprising approximately **115,000** names, or **123,000** altogether. The lists for the Southern States were very meagre, that for Louisiana, for example, consisting only of the city of New Orleans, while the list for Alabama was confined to the city of Mobile. The fact that any lists at all for these States were included at this early date speaks volumes for the energy and enterprise of the publishers. The Key alluded to in the last paragraph of the preface, was as follows:

KEY.

PECUNIARY STRENGTH.		GENERAL CREDIT.
(Left-hand column.)		(Right-hand column.)

	PECUNIARY STRENGTH		GENERAL CREDIT	
A1+	$1,000,000 or over.		A1	Unlimited
A1	500,000 to 1,000,000		1	
1	250,000 to 500,000		1½	High
1½	100,000 to 250,000			
2	50,000 to 100,000		2	
2½	25,000 to 50,000		2½	Good
3	10,000 to 25,000		3	
3½	5,000 to 10,000		3½	Fair

? Inquire at our Office.*

The first Key in which the present system of "markings" was adopted. Although since greatly improved and extended, this Key is the prototype of all its successors

In the 1864 edition the name of the publishers appears as R. G. Dun & Co. for the first time, the style for 1859 having been B. Douglass & Co. and for 1860 and 1861, Dun, Boyd & Co. On August 1st, 1864, the Montreal office published a special Reference Book for the British Provinces in pocket size, the pages being 4 inches wide by 6⅜ high. This book contained 494 pages and about 14,000 names, and was evidently sold to subscribers in the United States who desired Canadian ratings, as well as to those in Canada, as these ratings were omitted from the general reference books above described. The Key in the Canadian book was substantially the same as the one printed in the general Reference Book, except that in the left-hand column the figure 4 was added, to indicate pecuniary strength between $2,000 and $5,000. A second edition of the Canadian book was issued August 25th, 1865, with approximately 16,250 names.

The Reference Book for January, 1866, was substantially like that for 1865, except that the Key contained a 4 in the left-hand column, as in the Canadian books. This edition contained approximately 16,250 names for New York City and Brooklyn, and about 135,500 for the rest of the United States. The editions of 1864, 1865 and 1866 had brown leather backs, like those of the earlier editions, but green cloth sides similar to the ones used now.

On July 1st, 1866, a second edition of the Reference Book for that year was published, and the announcement made that thereafter the work would be issued semi-annually. In this volume the Southern States were fully reported for the first time since the war—the earlier volume for 1866 containing only the principal cities. The number of names in this volume was approximately 200,000. This edition was very favorably received by the leading New York journals, as the following interesting extracts from their notices of that year show:

From the *New York Express.*—The information which this work contains is of great interest and value, and its reliability thoroughly guaranteed by the fact that nearly all our leading merchants and bankers have for years liberally sustained this Agency.

From the *Financial Chronicle.*—This volume is a very remarkable one, whether regarded in the light of usefulness to the business community or of the labor and research of which it is the result. It contains a statement of the capital of almost every business man in the United States, with an indication of the general credit of each individual. The labor necessary to obtain this information must have been very great, since there are in the book Two Hundred Thousand names, each of which, of course, has to be the subject of special investigation. Messrs. Dun & Co. have long been engaged in this business and their reports have proved to be so reliable that they have won the confidence of the commercial community.

From the *New York Daily Tribune.*—"The Mercantile Agency" is an institution which has been in successful operation in this city during the last twenty-five years. . . . The talents, energy and enterprise uniformly displayed in its various managements, have brought The Mercantile Agency to a magnitude and importance that could scarcely have been conceived of by the Messrs. Tappan, its original founders. The "Reference Book" is put forth as an important auxiliary to the general business of the office. It is a brief synopsis of the information which is spread out, in detail, upon the Records of the Agency, and which, in many cases, runs back through the entire period of twenty-five years. The book is evidently the result of immense labor and of a large outlay of capital. . . . As we turn over its pages we can determine, at a glance, the commercial strength and importance of each town and city, but, when the objects of its publication are taken into account, and regarded in the light of its advantages to the banking, mercantile and manufacturing interests, its value becomes incalculable, for it contains what could not be gathered from any other source.

From the *Journal of Commerce.*—Considering the work in all its bearings, as a succinct statement of capital employed in the various branches of trade, and of the general condition of mercantile credit, also showing at a glance the relative commercial importance of towns and cities (thereby affording bankers and merchants essential aid in determining the extent of their credits), we cannot but esteem this Reference Book as a business publication of the highest value, and no doubt it will be regarded as a standard work by the mercantile community.

From the *Banker's Magazine.*—This is a remarkable work in many respects. It contains the names of nearly every merchant, manufacturer and trader in the United

States, some 200,000 in number, to which are attached figures indicating the capital and credit standing of each person. The labor expended in ascertaining this information must have been immense. It has necessitated the employment of an army of reporters, travelers, correspondents and clerks, and is, doubtless, as the publishers say, the result of the closest application and observation for a great many years. . . . The system of marking or rating is peculiar to the Agency, and is manifestly superior to any other method yet originated in its definiteness and simplicity. . . . If MESSRS. R. G. DUN & Co. were not thoroughly satisfied as to the general reliability of their information, they would hardly be bold enough to issue such a book as this, and place it in the hands of the entire trade. Indeed, the Agency is now almost universally acknowledged essential to any business in which even short credits are an element. We commend this volume to our mercantile and banking friends in the city and country.

Similar comments were also published in the *New York Times* and the *New York Evening Post*— the entire series forming a very interesting and remarkable group of contemporary opinions as to the merits of the book and the care and thoroughness with which it had been compiled.

In 1867, or soon afterward, the appearance of the Reference Book was considerably changed. The editions in the late sixties were bound in green cloth covers, but by the early seventies the publishers had adopted the red leather backs and corners and the green cloth sides that have been a feature of every subsequent edition and are now familiar wherever The Mercantile Agency's Reference Book is known. The January, 1867, issue contained 225,000 names and included Canada, for the first time since the war, the Canadian books having previously been published in the small pocket size adopted in 1864. This edition also had a list of the national banks of the United States established between 1863 and 1866. The total number of ratings in the July book was approximately 300,000.

During 1868 the growth of the book continued, January being considerably larger than the previous July, while the edition for July, 1868, was stated in the preface to contain "very nearly Four Hundred Thousand Names and Ratings, comprising almost every person engaged in Mercantile or Manufacturing Pursuits throughout the Union and Provinces." In this issue a most important change was made in the Key by substituting capital letters for figures in the left-hand column. The reason for the change is stated in the preface as follows: "We found not unfrequently that these figures led to confusion in the minds of Subscribers, many of whom failed to comprehend that the same character in different columns, had an entirely different signification. In order, therefore, to make our system of marking more definite, we have substituted letters in the first column, by which we convey Estimates of Capital, retaining the Figures in the second column, by which we convey Indications of Credit." As this important change made the left-hand column substantially what it is to-day, the Key, as it appears in the July, 1868, book, is reprinted herewith in full just as it then appeared:

Key to Left-Hand Column.		Key to Right-Hand Column.	
PECUNIARY STRENGTH.		**GENERAL CREDIT.**	
A+ (A1+) - - Over $1,000,000		**A1,** - - - - - Unlimited.	
A (A1)- - - Over 500,000			
B (1) - - - Over 250,000		**1** }	
C (1½) - - Over 100,000		**1½** } - - - - - High.	
D (2) - - - Over 50,000			
E (2½) - - Over 25,000		**2** }	
F (3) - - - Over 10,000		**2½** } - - - - - Good.	
G (3½) - - Over 5,000			
H (4) - - Over 2,000		**3** }	
K - - - - Less than 2,000		**3½** } - - - - - Fair.	

From 1869 onward the number of ratings in the Reference Book increased steadily year by year, the only notable decrease for many years being in 1873, when the first book issued did not appear until February, owing to a fire in the printing plant. How promptly and effectively this emergency was met is thus described in the preface to that volume:

Within thirty clear working days a feat in typography has been performed, which, if we mistake not, has never been equaled in this or any other country. It has been accomplished only by combining the facilities of eight of the largest printing establishments of the country—one in Philadelphia, one in Boston and six in New York, who, with type founders, papermakers and bookbinders, have done their utmost to aid us in our emergency.

The back of the title-page contains the list of plants at which the book was printed, as follows:

Printed in part by J. B. Lippincott, Philadelphia, Pa.; H. O. Houghton & Co., Cambridge, Mass.; D. Appleton & Co., Pool & McLaughlin & Co., David H. Gildersleeve, Francis Hart & Co., Wynkoop & Hallenbeck, S. W. Green, and Dun, Barlow & Co., all of New York.

In this edition the shape of the book was somewhat altered, the pages being made wider, so as to accommodate four columns of names instead of three, and somewhat longer, with the result that a page of solid matter in the 1873 book contained 584 names as compared with 399 in the smaller size previously issued. The July, 1873, book was printed entirely in the firm's own printing plant, and beginning with that issue it was announced that the Reference Book would thereafter be issued four times a year—in January, March, July and September.

As it would be tedious to describe in detail each of the many Reference Books issued from the early seventies down to the present time, the following table has been prepared to show at a glance the steady progress from year to year in the number of ratings printed. For the sake of completeness the table includes all years from 1859 to 1916:

Year	Number	Year	Number	Year	Number
1859	20,268	1879	737,804	1899	1,241,591
1860	31,278	1880	764,000	1900	1,285,816
1861	25,560	1881	806,000	1901	1,291,892
1862	not issued	1882	848,000	1902	1,309,410
1863	not issued	1883	890,000	1903	1,382,640
1864	123,000	1884	933,159	1904	1,422,048
1865	123,000	1885	982,993	1905	1,443,241
1866	141,750	1886	1,025,000	1906	1,483,579
1867	225,000	1887	1,071,055	1907	1,524,383
1868	350,000	1888	1,103,299	1908	1,554,431
1869	400,000	1889	1,135,036	1909	1,587,977
1870	430,573	1890	1,176,988	1910	1,632,460
1871	486,023	1891	1,203,516	1911	1,670,825
1872	532,000	1892	1,239,424	1912	1,705,952
1873	525,000	1893	1,294,786	1913	1,797,401
1874	594,189	1894	1,299,091	1914	1,816,737
1875	641,239	1895	1,298,169	1915	1,844,506
1876	680,072	1896	1,320,251	1916	*1,882,226
1877	691,154	1897	1,248,298	1916	†1,899,490
1878	713,420	1898	1,251,314	* January.	† July.

Among the more noteworthy changes and improvements effected in the Reference Books since 1874, the following merit special mention. In the January, 1877, book the Key was again changed, the left-hand column being considerably extended, while in the right-hand column the word "Unlimited" was changed to "Very High."

EXPLANATORY KEY

TO THE

LEFT-HAND COLUMN.		RIGHT-HAND COLUMN.	
ESTIMATED PECUNIARY STRENGTH		**GENERAL CREDIT.**	
AA	- - $1,000,000 or over.	A1	- - - - - Very High.
A+	- - - 750,000 or over.		
A	- - - 500,000 to $750,000		
B+	- - - 300,000 to 500,000	1	
B	- - - 150,000 to 300,000	1½ }	- - - - - - High.
C	- - - 75,000 to 150,000		
D	- - - 40,000 to 75,000		
E	- - - 20,000 to 40,000	2	
F	- - - 10,000 to 20,000	2½ }	- - - - - Good.
G	- - 5,000 to 10,000		
H	- - - 2,000 to 5,000		
K	- - 1,000 to 2,000	3	
L	- - - — to 1,000	3½ }	- - - - - Fair.

The absence of a Rating indicates those whose business and investments render it difficult to rate them satisfactorily to ourselves. We therefore prefer, in justice to these, to give our detailed report on record at our offices.

The present Key is considerably more elaborate than this, containing 17 symbols, instead of 13, to indicate pecuniary strength; and 48, as compared with 7, to indicate general credit. In its main principles, however, it is the same as the one printed above, so that no further allusion to this topic will be necessary.

In the book for January, 1880, the size was once more increased to accommodate five columns of names and ratings to a page. In this book, also, estimates of population were inserted for the first time under the name of the town with an indication as to whether it was a banking town and if not, the name of the most convenient banking town. In addition to 41,500 post offices this book contained the names of every railroad station throughout the United States and Canada, or 65,000 places in all, together with the delivering express company at each station. In the March, 1886, book appeared the first installment of a series of State maps, the preface stating that "the need of a ready reference to the immediate locality of places and their geographical location, in shipping goods and in correspondence, is constantly being sought by merchants and those who are dispensing credit." This valuable feature has been continued ever since both for the United States and Canada. In March, 1885, the Reference Book for the first time contained symbols to indicate classifications of trade, a Key on the inside of the front cover explaining the system. This plan proved to be a very great success and has since been a feature of all Reference Books published by The Mercantile Agency.

The early Canadian Reference Books, published by the Montreal and later by the Toronto offices, beginning in 1864, may be looked upon as the first pocketbooks in the history of the Agency. These have been continued in pocket size, ever since, although after 1867 the Canadian names were also printed in the large Reference Books as well. Beginning in the early seventies, the first pocketbooks covering portions of the United States were issued, and the series has been continually enlarged until, at present, it comprises 56 books altogether, covering every State separately and also the cities of Chicago, Boston, St. Louis, New York and Philadelphia.

When it is considered that the present Reference Book contains close to one million, nine hundred thousand names, as compared with twenty thousand in the edition of 1859, it will readily be realized that the compilation, printing and publishing of so huge a book four times a year is a task of extraordinary magnitude and complexity. This department of The Mercantile Agency has been developed to a very high degree of efficiency. The Reference Book to-day is printed with all possible despatch and, by a carefully prepared system, all changes occurring throughout the United States and Canada are made up to a few minutes of the closing of a particular State, Territory or Province. In a great many cases, where changes are of special importance, they are made while the other portions of the same State, Territory, or Province are being printed. This necessitates personal and experienced supervision, but no task is deemed too arduous for this all-important work. In less than eight hours after the complete book has been printed several hundred copies have already been bound, boxed, shipped and are on the fast express trains taking them to the leading distributing centers throughout the districts for which they are destined.

101

While the table on page 98 shows the steady increase in the number of names in the various Reference Books from 1859 down to the present time, it really conveys a very inadequate conception of the enormous amount of labor and detail involved in the preparation and publication of these great volumes. From the standpoint of increase in the number of ratings alone a more instructive comparison would be by decades, as follows:

Year	Number of Names	Increase		
1859	20,268			
1868	350,000	Increase over	1859	329,732
1878	713,420	” ”	1868	363,420
1888	1,103,299	” ”	1878	389,879
1898	1,251,314	” ”	1888	148,015
1908	1,554,383	” ”	1898	303,069
1916 (eight years)	1,882,226	” ”	1908	327,843

Even this table does not adequately represent the amount of work accomplished, because the net increases do not indicate how many names were obliterated, or the number of corrections made in ratings, firm styles, or in the bank list.

This is clearly shown in the following table, which gives the total number of annual changes made during the last five calendar years:

	1911.	1912.	1913.	1914.	1915.
New names inserted	392,293	404,857	417,065	416,347	407,072
Names obliterated.	348,332	345,668	359,654	374,230	377,246
Changes in ratings and styles....	381,701	396,260	434,350	449,443	441,126
Alterations in bank list..........	64,621	65,909	74,414	79,845	85,081
Total number of Changes......	1,186,947	1,212,694	1,285,483	1,319,865	1,310,525
Average for each business day..	3,916	3,989	4,214	4,356	4,325

In other words, while the net gain between the January Reference Book of 1911 and that for

January, 1916—five years later—was **123,578** names, the total number of changes of all kinds made during these years amounted to **6,315,514,** or three and one-half times the average number of names in the Reference Book during this period. In order to keep pace with the steady increase in this immense amount of detail work, the Printing Department has had to be successively enlarged several times, and particulars regarding the present modern and up-to-date printing house and bindery of The Mercantile Agency will be found in the last chapter of this book. The preceding sketch of the history of the Reference Book has been brought down to date at this point as a matter of convenience, thus avoiding the repetition that would be involved in tracing its progress and growth from decade to decade since it was first established fifty-seven years ago.

From 1859 to 1865 no new branch offices of The Mercantile Agency were established—the only period in the history of the institution when more than three years elapsed without witnessing a single extension of the Agency's chain. The reason was, of course, the Civil War, which retarded the nation's industrial and commercial growth for five years. In 1865 the styles of the Baltimore and Richmond offices—which were originally opened as J. D. Pratt & Co.—were changed to R. G. DUN & Co., thus making the firm style of all the offices of The Mercantile Agency in the United States R. G. DUN & Co., with the exception of the Boston district. On January 1st, 1866,

Erastus Wiman, then general manager in Canada, was called to New York and succeeded to the position formerly occupied by Robert B. Boyd, who retired in the early sixties. While the volume of its business was greatly reduced during the Civil War, prudent management enabled the Agency to pass through that critical period successfully, and now that peace was restored the expansion of the organization was quickly resumed. In 1866 an office was opened at Buffalo, then a city of less than 70,000 inhabitants. The first manager of the new branch asked for $300 for expenses, and with this small sum put it on a self-supporting basis. He made the trip from Schenectady to Buffalo on foot, carrying a Reference Book under his arm in order to show it to merchants along the way —the long tramp resulting in quite a number of subscribers. In 1867, despite the commercial prostration of the South, an office was opened at Memphis, Tenn., a convincing evidence of the firm's faith in the

Buffalo Office, established 1866
The office at present occupies the entire ground floor of the Dun Building

recuperative powers of that section. Memphis at that time was hardly more than a fair-sized country town, and the territory reported was largely forest and plantation property, with dirt roads, over which travel was necessarily by horseback.

In 1868 four new offices were established—the largest number for a single year in the history of the Agency down to that time. At Portland, Maine, E. Russell & Co., of Boston, established a branch to

take care of their subscribers in that State, as well as to give more thorough work in reporting. The business of The Mercantile Agency in Canada was greatly stimulated as a result of Confederation, which took place in 1867, and the energy with

Albany Office, established 1868
A portion of the main office, on the sixth floor of the Hun Building

which merchants at Montreal, Toronto and Quebec extended their trade into all parts of Nova Scotia and New Brunswick—which were then united with the Dominion—necessitated a new office at Halifax, N. S., in 1868, while one was opened at St. John, N. B., three years later. At that time the principles and objects of The Mercantile Agency were little understood in the maritime provinces, and for a time there was some misunderstanding as to the purposes of the institution. The Halifax office has kept a scrap-book from the date of its establishment to the present time, which contains many of the early criticisms, and also editorials by leading journals retracting what had been said and commending the Agency after they had come to know it more thoroughly. The other offices opened in 1868 were Toledo, Ohio, and Albany, N. Y.

In April, 1869, an office was established at San Francisco—the first branch of The Mercantile Agency west of the Rocky Mountains. The ter-ritory included in the San Francisco district was a vast empire, em-bracing the present States of California, Nevada, Utah, Mon-tana, Oregon a n d Washington, together

Halifax Office, established 1868
Where the firm now occupy rooms on the
third floor of the Royal Bank Building

with British Columbia. At the outset, the recep-tion accorded to the new enterprise was discourag-ing. The majority of the principal merchants at San Francisco felt that the Agency could be of little benefit to them since their credit customers were made up chiefly of what they called "support accounts." By this they meant that their customers were practically controlled by them, and that they knew all about their financial affairs. This situation was one that, with local modifications, confronted the managers of the pioneer offices of The Mercantile Agency in all parts of the West and Southwest. It could only be met by *proving* to the satisfaction of

San Francisco Office, established 1869
The present office is on the third floor of the Insurance Exchange Building

the leaders in each community that the information secured by the new institution was better and more complete than they themselves possessed, even about their own customers. By reason of its disinterested position the Agency often ascertained facts that the wholesale houses, being interested parties, never learned. The thorough and systematic manner in which it collected and verified its data proved to be a great improvement over the usual practice of the banking and trading houses of those days, and it was not long before influential firms, which had at first held aloof, voluntarily became subscribers, and have

107

ever since continued to be its loyal friends. At San Francisco, and at the various other pioneer offices in the vast region beyond the Mississippi now being rapidly opened up for settlement, the Agency won its way by demonstrating the value of its service, and accepting any tests that those most familiar with local conditions cared to apply as to the accuracy of its information. Many of the minor offices in the more sparsely settled portions of this region have never been self-supporting, but have been maintained at a loss year after year in order to provide the mercantile community at the larger trading centers with the prompt and reliable information without which credit business in those localities would be impossible.

Rochester Office, established 1870
At present occupying the east half of the fifth floor of the Insurance Building

One other office was established in 1869, at Norfolk, Va., and two in 1870—at Rochester, N. Y., and Hartford, Conn. Each of these branches gave the organization an extension in territory where its services were needed—that at Hartford, for example, resulting in the opening of new suboffices in quick succession at Providence, New Haven and Springfield, Mass., early in the next decade.

Altogether, during the period from 1859 to 1870, ten new branches of the Agency were established—an excellent showing considering the profound disturbance to the nation's mercantile activities occasioned by the war. The most notable achievement of these eleven years, however, was the inauguration of the Reference Book, which by the close of the period was firmly established as an indispensable adjunct to credit transactions in every part of the United States and Canada.

Hartford Office, established 1870
Occupying half of the third floor of the
Hartford Life Insurance Building

The extension of the service of the Agency to the Pacific coast during this troubled period is also of interest, especially as the opening of the San Francisco office preceded the completion of the first transcontinental railway, which was then slowly creeping up to the summit of the Rockies from both sides. By the close of 1870 The Mercantile Agency had entirely recov-

ered from the retarding influences of the war and was
ready to keep pace with the swift development of the
nation's vast natural resources that followed the opening of millions of fertile acres to settlement as new
railways advanced into the interior in every direction.

CHAPTER V

The Agency Keeps Pace With the Nation's Growth

1871–1890

THE fourth and fifth decades in the history of The Mercantile Agency were periods of unexampled expansion, no less than fifty new offices being established between 1871 and 1880, and forty-eight between 1881 and 1890. Of these, ninety were in the United States, four in Canada, three in Europe and one in Australia, so that the most noteworthy feature of these years was the enormous extension of the organization within the United States. The opening of these new branches came about in two ways. Many of them were decided upon by the executive administration at New York for the purpose of carrying the service of the Agency into regions where it had previously been little known. Others were started by the district managers—with the consent of the New York executives—as sub-offices to enable them to give more prompt and efficient service in the territory under their control. In each case the new offices were the Agency's response to the fast-growing requirements of the business community throughout the United States, and the increase in their number from 28 to 126 in two decades shows how closely the institution kept pace with the nation's growth.

Until 1870 the paralyzing influence of the great war was still felt in all branches of the country's industrial and mercantile activities. Railroad building, which had been advancing apace during the fifties, practically ceased from 1861 to 1865, and was resumed haltingly and slowly. Capital found its way back into the channels of trade timidly at first. Then, with a sudden wave of the optimism that in America seems to be more buoyant and all-pervading than anywhere else, the great nation, reunited, started on its forward course. The completion of the first transcontinental railroad on May 10th, 1869, stirred the imagination of the whole country and of the world. For twenty years the army of California gold seekers had gone around the stormy Horn, across the deadly Isthmus, or had slowly followed the long and weary trails across the continent, exposed to incessant dangers from Indians and to no small risk of destruction from thirst and starvation. Now the prairie schooner gave way to the express train, and the entire Pacific Slope began to fill up, as well as the vast region on both sides of the 1,800 miles of single-track line from Council Bluffs to San Francisco, which was thus thrown open to settlement. Europe began to send its capital to develop the wealth of America's vast western territories, while immigrants by hundreds of thousands began to flock to this New World of unbounded opportunity.

It is interesting to note how this spirit of optimism was reflected in the growth of The Mercantile Agency. In 1871 six new offices were opened —more than in any single year since the institution started. In 1872 no less than twenty new branches were established. Here is the list for 1871, in the order in which they are listed in the Red Book:* Nashville, Tenn.; St. John, N. B.; Indianapolis, Ind.; Newark, N. J.; Portland, Ore., and Providence, R. I. There was one office in the South, one in the British Provinces, one in t h e Central States, o n e in the C e n t r a l Atlantic States, one o n the Pacific Slope and one in New England—if the managers of the Agency h a d wished

Providence Office, established 1871
Facing Exchange Place, the civic center of this busy industrial city

to demonstrate how skillfully they could meet the growing needs of every part of the United States and Canada, they could hardly have made a better distribution. The office at Nashville, originally opened from Louisville, is now the head of a very extensive district of its own; the branch at St.

*The Red Book is a publication of some 220 pages for the use of branch managers. It gives the list of offices, alphabetically, chronologically, by districts, etc., and the exact territory assigned to each, the office responsible for each county, etc.

John was opened by the Montreal office as a result of the union of the maritime provinces with Canada; the Indianapolis office was at first in the Cincinnati district, but is now independent, while Newark was opened directly from New York. Providence was at first a suboffice of Hartford.

At Portland, Ore., then a suboffice in the San Francisco district, the manager had to face veritable pioneering conditions in 1871. The city had a population of 8,203, and was the only place of importance in the entire Pacific Northwest. It therefore enjoyed a wholesale trade out of all proportion to its size and had many prosperous merchants. The only railroad in Oregon at that time ran from Portland to Roseburg, a distance of 198 miles. In Washington Territory the Northern Pacific had built a line from Kalama to Tacoma, a distance of 102 miles, with a branch from Tenino Junction to Olympia, some 15 miles. There was also a primitive line from Walla Walla to Wallula, about 31 miles in length. Everywhere else in Oregon, with its area of 96,030 square miles, and in Washington with 69,180, traveling was by primitive river boats and by stage. In the winter the almost bottomless roads rendered progress slow and uncertain, while in summer the thick dust was almost equally unpleasant. The population was sparse and the towns few and far between. One traveler covered the entire district at first, and made trips of magnificent distances. Starting at Ashland, near the California line, he went by stage to Roseburg, about

Portland, Ore., Office, established 1871
First opened when Portland had a population of 8,203.
The present office is located in the Morgan Building

140 miles. Thence the trip to Portland down the Willamette Valley could be made by rail, and from there to The Dalles, on the Columbia River, by steamboat. From that point the trip had to be made by "buckboard" to Canyon City, 350 miles in the interior and most of the way out of sight of settlements. Then followed trips by stage, buckboard or on horseback of 55, 96, 173, 292, and 220 miles, and a final long river stretch of 356 miles back to Portland, making a total circuit of nearly 1,800 miles! In Washington the traveler's task was nearly as arduous, and he also had to go across the Sound to report British Columbia.

The number of offices opened in 1872 was so great that individual references to each of them would be tedious. Those selected for illustration in this chapter

115

are district offices at present.   The list follows:

Columbus, Ohio	Quincy, Ill.
Davenport, Iowa	St. Joseph, Mo.
Dayton, Ohio	Scranton, Pa.
Dubuque, Iowa	Syracuse, N. Y.
Erie, Pa.	Troy, N. Y.
Evansville, Ind.	Utica, N. Y.
Galveston, Texas	Worcester, Mass.
Grand Rapids, Mich.	Glasgow, Scotland.
Kansas City, Mo.	Paris, France
Mobile, Ala.	Hamilton, Ont.

Denver Office, established 1874
Occupying about half of the 7th floor
of the Exchange Building

T h e opening of the Galveston office illustrates the shift in mercantile conditions, due to the rapid expansion of the country, that resulted in the establishment of m a n y new branch offices d u r i n g this period. As the railroads did not begin to reach into Texas from the North and East until after the close of t h e war, Galveston was, down to t h e middle sixties, about the only commercial gateway to the State. Merchandise came to the port by coasting steamers and nearly all business transactions of any moment had their origin at New Orleans, where The Mercantile Agency had maintained an office since 1851. With the increase in population in the vast region comprised within the boundaries of Texas, independent distributing houses began to be established at Galveston and commercial relations with New Orleans dwindled rapidly. The opening of the Galveston office was, therefore, a prompt recognition on the part of the executive management of the altered mercantile situation in this district.

The next to the last office in the large group established in 1872—that at Paris— also merits a brief word in passing. Opened almost simultaneously with the

Glasgow Office, established 1872
Situated in Castle Chambers,
55 West Regent Street

suboffice established by the London branch at Glasgow, it was the third branch of The Mercantile Agency in Europe. For twenty years the office supplied international service only—reporting to New York and London regarding the standing of French houses, and to clients in France regarding credits in the other regions covered by The Mercantile Agency. It was not until after the year 1900 that the Paris office began to assume the important place in the Agency system that it holds to-day.

In 1873, the year of the great panic, only one new office was established, that at New Haven, Conn., which was originally opened as a suboffice of Hartford. During the next four years, however, the expansion of the service was so rapid that the list of the new offices can best be indicated by a table:

In 1874.	In 1876.
Atlanta, Ga.	La Crosse, Wis.
Denver, Col.	Berlin, Germany
Savannah, Ga.	London, Ont.
Williamsport, Pa.	In 1877.
In 1875.	Minneapolis, Minn.
Gloversville, N. Y.	Omaha, Neb.
Dallas, Tex.	Peoria, Ill.
St. Paul, Minn.	Springfield, Mass.
Houston, Tex.	Des Moines, Iowa.
Keokuk, Iowa	
Binghamton, N. Y.	

The second office in the 1874 group was another pioneer in a new district. The following brief account of the conditions under which the work of the Agency was carried on at that point forty-two years ago is of interest, because the conditions described were in a general way similar to those encountered at most of the offices established in the West and Southwest during the period:

> The town (Denver) at that time was rough and tough, and had a population of about 25,000. It was a mining and cattle center. It grew rapidly, however, and our office with it. . . . During the period from 1880 to 1890 the town experienced a terrific boom and the work of The Mercantile Agency in those days was

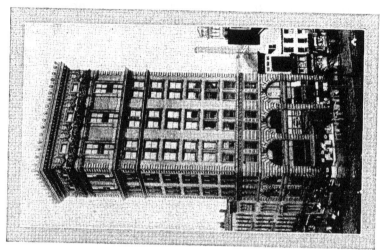

Dayton, Ohio, Office
Conover Building

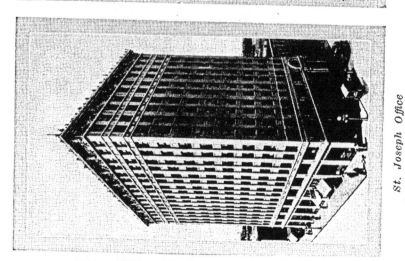

Quincy, Ill., Office
Illinois State Bank Building

St. Joseph Office
Corby-Forsee Building

Three of the twenty branch offices of The Mercantile Agency established in 1872

one of great difficulty and responsibility. Merchants, traders and other people came from all parts of the country, started in business, and immediately sought credit. Reliable credit information, as can be readily understood, was very difficult to secure under the circumstances.

The same remarks apply to other parts of the territory which was then, and is now, under the jurisdiction of this office. Prosperous towns like Leadville and Cripple Creek sprang up almost over night, huge ore bodies were discovered and immense wealth was created in a few weeks—bringing with it all its attending parasites. The merchants and manufacturers in the East, who made large fortunes out of their Western business, do not give The Mercantile Agency credit for the wonderful work it performed in their interest in those days, or realize how steadfastly and persistently it separated, in a credit way, the wolves from the lambs, and the sheep from the goats.

Men would walk down the main street of the city of Leadville swinging their revolvers by a chain attached to their wrists, ready for use on the slightest provocation. Shooting scrapes in a gambling "joint" next to our office were a regular occurrence. During that entire period, we always had traveling reporters to cover the territory. The arduousness of their work can well be imagined. Railroads and trains were few and far between; most of the traveling had to be done on horseback or by stage through the ranches, hills and mining towns in sparsely settled districts infested by desperadoes, half-breeds, cowpunchers and tough characters of all kinds. Stage robberies were frequent and the rights of property were often decided either by the fitful laws of chance, or by quickness on the trigger.

In connection with the early history of the office at La Crosse, Wis., a report of the establishment of the office, which appeared in the *Daily Liberal Democrat* of La Crosse, February 7th, 1876, contained the following interesting paragraph:

This Agency has always been active in initiating and putting in improvements whenever and wherever there has seemed to be need of any. They have recently brought to their aid the new invention called Type Writing Machines, by which all of their reports are manifolded and at once duplicated to every office in the chain—68 in all. This does away with the former delay of having to send to some branch office for the required information.

This reference to the use of the typewriter is especially interesting, because it indicates at what an early date that invention was in general use in the offices of The Mercantile Agency, which was the first great American business house to give this device a practical trial. The first experiments with the typewriter began in the winter of 1866-67. Altogether, some twenty-five or thirty experimental machines were

Omaha Office
Established 1877
Woodmen of the World Building

constructed, "each a little better than its predecessor though still lacking the essentials of a successful machine." In 1873 a few of the first model that seemed to be commercially practicable were made and offered to the public, but it proved to be very hard to interest capital in the new invention. In 1874 the device was shown to the New York executives of R. G. Dun & Co., who agreed that if it could be demonstrated that the machines were capable of accomplishing certain results the firm would supply the means

to build some of them and would give the invention a thorough trial. There was then no such thing as carbon paper and the first experiments in manifolding were made by using shoe blacking smeared over thin manila paper. After several months of experimenting the work produced by these crude methods was shown to the management of The Mercantile Agency and an

St. Paul Office
Established 1875
Commerce Building

order was placed for 100 machines to be distributed among the various offices. This was the first large order secured by the inventors and their associates, and came at the critical moment when the writing machine was struggling for general recognition and the enterprise seemed doomed to failure from lack of public support.

The machine thus adopted was a clumsy looking affair, compared with the visible writing machines of the present day. The front, back and sides were entirely enclosed with enameled tin, and the keyboard

The first typewriter used in the work of The Mercantile Agency—afterwards known as "Remington Model No. 1"

had a hinged cover. While the machines were being manufactured, experiments were made with a view to producing a black paper that could be used between two sheets of white paper that would leave

A portion of a page in one of the oldest record books of the Agency, reduced about one-half, showing the beautiful penmanship of those early days

an impression on the white paper when struck by a type. Success attended these efforts and a firm in Philadelphia began to supply carbon paper, or "black impression paper," as it was at first called, in sufficient quantities to meet the requirements of the Agency. Several months were necessary in order to complete the machines, and it was 1875 before everything was ready for the test of actual use in the every-day work of the organization. There are a number of the employees in some of the older offices who can still recall the advent of the "new-fangled contraption" for doing away with handwriting and the laborious copying of reports. Naturally the best penmen were strongly opposed to the machine at first and some of them reported that it was "no good." Gradually, however (and largely as a result of the practical tests applied in the work of the Agency), the early imperfections and crudities of the original machine were eliminated and the operators became more proficient.

It is possible, by referring to the early archives of The Mercantile Agency, to fix with considerable definiteness the date when the typewriter was adopted for general use throughout all the branch offices of the institution. On November 23rd, 1875, the firm sent out a circular to all its branch managers, giving them final instructions as to "Duplication by Manifolding." This was accompanied by a book of 153 pages containing 21 pages of Rules and Instructions relative to the use of the typewriter in manifolding tissue copies of all reports. The remaining pages contained the distribution tables for each of the 65 offices in existence at that time. This was the first edition of the "Distribution Tables," a feature of the Agency system that has been continued ever since. The first and second editions, the latter issued in 1877, were bound in green covers, but for many years past the book has been bound in blue covers, and is now generally known as the Blue Book. The following extract from the 1875 edition explains the purpose of the new system:

> The "Original" copy of a report has hitherto served a very important purpose, for, after having been copied in the office of origin, it has been sent to the nearest office demanding the information, and, after copying, by them transmitted to others, and so on, to whatever office required to copy the territory from which the report originated. But it has been found that from the multiplication of offices which the last few years has witnessed, and also from the changes which new railroads and the creation of new markets have made, that this mode of depending upon the original document to supply all the demands for information from it, is utterly inadequate. Hence a necessity has arisen for some mode by which a report originating in one office should be simultaneously and promptly distributed to all Branches that need the information. . . .
>
> One of the objects sought by duplication is to enable . . . all the offices to make, by aid of the typewriter and manifold paper, as many copies of every report as will be required by the various offices interested therein, and transmitting the same simultaneously to them.

Another object of the new plan was to do away entirely with the copying in longhand of the enormous number of reports required by other offices, as it was proposed that thereafter "the copies of reports

Springfield, Mass., Office (1877)
Stearns Building

Indianapolis Office (1871)
State Life Building

Between 1871 and 1877 no less than 42 offices were opened in the United States and Canada

New Haven Office (1873)
Second National Bank Building

shall reach offices that need them in such shape that they can be pasted in Binders or Scrap-books specially prepared for the purpose, so that the reports may be not only safely preserved, but be made readily accessible." This system of duplication by manifolding was gradually extended to all the offices in the Agency's chain and there can be very little doubt that

A portion of the Winnipeg office in the Keewayden Building.
This branch was opened in 1882

The Mercantile Agency was the largest individual user of typewriters at that date.

Prior to the introduction of the typewriter the records of every office were kept in substantially the same way as those of Lewis Tappan & Co. in 1841— in huge ledgers, each item being copied in longhand. The handwriting in these old records was almost uniformly excellent, and in many cases even beautiful, but the system was cumbersome and laborious. Whenever an office was burned, or a new office opened, many thousands of these records had to be copied from the books of other offices into a new set of ledgers. As the number of records increased the task of indexing this vast amount of information became a well-nigh colossal one, for frequently the records of a

Half of the main room of the St. Paul Office,
which occupies 4,000 square feet altogether

single concern might be entered in a dozen different volumes. From constant handling, moreover, the ledgers soon became dilapidated and in time had to be re-copied. There are volumes in the possession of the head office at New York in which records dated 1846 are written on the same page with others as late as 1870. It was the universal practice in the early days to invite subscribers to call at the offices and have reports in which they were interested read to them. In New York it was the custom of large merchants, like A. T. Stewart & Co., to have a trusted clerk from the credit department at the office of the Agency all day long, while many concerns had clerks who spent half their time there. The adoption of the typewriter enabled the Agency to save to its subscribers the entire time of these clerks—in many instances amounting to hundreds or even thousands of dollars annually.

The adoption of the typewriter not only did away with all the copying of records by hand—thus doing away with the ledgers above described—but enabled the managers of the Agency to work out a new system for handling and filing reports. During the forty years that have elapsed since typewriting took the place of handwriting in the copying of the Agency's records many important improvements have been effected in the system first adopted, as explained in the 1875 edition of the Blue Book. It would be tedious to describe these changes in detail, but the following brief summary gives the essential facts regarding the system in operation in all offices of The Mercantile Agency throughout the world. One copy of every original report made in any office is sent to New York, and in the case of suboffices an additional copy is sent to the district office in charge. After these copies, or "tissues," as they are called, are received by the office where they are to be kept on file, they are pasted on heavy sheets of manila paper, each sheet having pasted upon it all the reports relating to a single firm. After the tissues fill both sides of the sheet others are added by means of linen hinges, so that in the case of a concern regarding which the records go back for many years the Agency may have scores of reports on file, all of which are kept together in the manner described, so that no reference to another set of sheets is necessary. The sheets are cut to a uniform size and put in binders, or compartments. As this system was inaugurated, and carried to a very high degree of perfection, long before modern office and filing appliances were thought of, the cases in which the binders are kept are not the same in all the offices — although the gen-

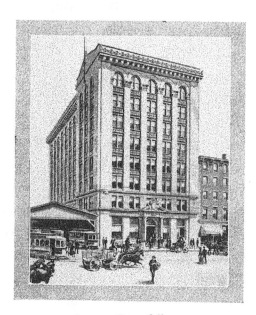

Jersey City Office
Established 1882
Commercial Trust Building

eral system of filing is identical. A number of the illustrations in this book show portions of the filing cabinets in use in various offices. It is difficult to convey an adequate conception of the enormous volume of mechanical work involved in copying, pasting and filing typewritten reports, and in making and delivering copies for subscribers and

131

other offices. Without the aid of the typewriter and the manifolding system it would be impossible for the Agency to keep abreast of the huge requirements of modern commerce, especially in the United States.

The next office established after that at La Crosse was located in Germany, and was opened in response to the demand for a branch of The Mercantile Agency in that country, owing to the rapid development of German commerce and industry after the conclusion of the war of 1870-71. This branch was first situated at Leipzig, the seat of the German fur trade and the principal commercial center of the Kingdom of Saxony. A few years later it was transferred to Berlin in consequence of the

Little Rock Office
Established 1879
Bank of Commerce Building

rapid growth of that city after it became the capital of the Empire. For a time the Berlin office confined itself chiefly to furnishing German subscribers with information regarding the standing of American firms, and supplying the other offices of the Agency chain with similar information for their subscribers regarding traders in Germany.

In 1878 only one new office was established, at Saginaw, Mich. At that time Saginaw was important

132

chiefly on account of its shipments of lumber and salt, the city being the center of the lumber industry of the State. The principal receipts from other points were sugar, coal and farm products. Curiously enough, the lumber industry is now a thing of the past, and the city's principal shipments are sugar, coal and farm products. In 1879 four new branches were opened— Allentown, Pa.; Bangor, Me.; Elmira, N. Y., and Little Rock, Ark. Among the correspondents of the Bangor office is an attorney whose father began to supply information to the Agency in his town in 1848 or 1849 and continued to act as correspondent there until his death, when he was succeeded by his son, who still acts in this capacity.

Jacksonville Office
Established 1890
Realty Building

In July, 1880, Charles Barlow, who had been a partner in the firm since 1859, died suddenly at his home at Long Branch, N. J. Mr. Barlow was born at Dudley, in Yorkshire, England, and entered the service of Lewis Tappan & Co. in 1844. Although only fifty-five years of age at the time of his death he had been in the employ of The Mercantile Agency thirty-six years. According to one of the obituary accounts of his career, "he was a man ardently devoted

133

to business, and was distinguished by a coolness and accuracy of judgment which made him a source of great strength to his house. He was conservative in his tendencies, but safe and sure." In the letter announcing his death the firm wrote: " His long years of devotedness to the best interests of the business, his sterling integrity and his remarkable capacity are now only recalled to mark how great has been our loss." The firm style of the New York office had been Dun, Barlow & Co. for many years, but after Mr. Barlow's death it was changed to R. G. DUN & Co., like the other offices in the United States and Europe. On January 1st, 1881, Robert Dun Douglass and A. J. King were admitted to partnership with Mr. Dun, and at the close of the following year- Matthias B. Smith retired.

In the year 1880 no new branch offices were opened, but in the decade from 1881 to 1890 the number of offices established was forty-eight, as follows:

1881
Salt Lake, Utah
Montgomery, Ala.
San Antonio, Tex.
Cedar Rapids, Iowa
Sioux City, Iowa

1882
Winnipeg, Man.
Fort Worth, Tex.
Reading, Pa.
Waco, Tex.
Jersey City, N. J.

1883
Lincoln, Neb.
Rockford, Ill.
Springfield, O.
Chattanooga, Tenn.
Austin, Tex.

1884
Knoxville, Tenn.
Ottumwa, Iowa
Duluth, Minn.

1885
Birmingham, Ala.

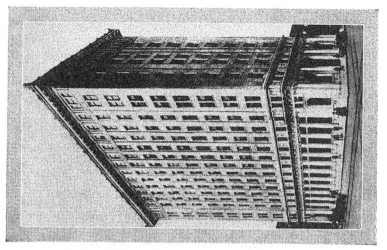

Knoxville Office (1884)
Holston National Bank Building

Los Angeles Office (1887)
International Bank Building

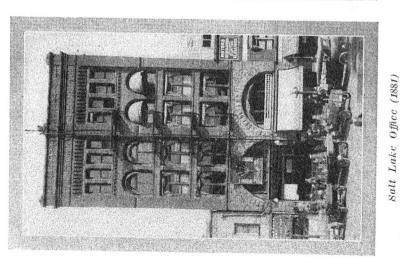

Salt Lake Office (1881)
Tribune and Western Union Building

In the decade from 1881 to 1890 the number of branch offices established was forty-eight

1886
Atchison, Kan.
Wheeling, W. Va.
Wichita, Kan.
Springfield, Mo.
Helena, Mont.
Sherman, Tex.
1887
Macon, Ga.
Los Angeles, Cal.
Sedalia, Mo.
Melbourne, Australia
1888
Shreveport, La.
Pueblo, Col.
Topeka, Kan.
Fort Smith, Ark.

Cairo, Ill.
Tacoma, Wash.
Seattle, Wash.
Spokane, Wash.
Wilmington, N. C.
El Paso, Tex.
1889
Wilmington, Del.
Bridgeport, Conn.
Paducah, Ky.
Columbus, Ga.
1890
Jacksonville, Fla.
Fort Wayne, Ind.
Lynchburg, Va.
Augusta, Ga.
Washington, D. C.

In many of these offices The Mercantile Agency, following the traditions of its earlier years, was with the vanguard of the pioneers who were then developing the vast resources of the West and Southwest in the United States and of Western Canada. In Texas the managers of the new offices frequently went out on the construction trains, arriving at their posts when the railroad did. Reporting these districts involved the same long journeys by river, rail, stagecoach and on horseback that characterized the work in the Far West. In Western Canada conditions were the same. When the Winnipeg office was opened in 1882, the manager, to reach his post, had to go by steamer to Duluth, then by rail as far as Glyndon, Minn. From that point he took a small steamer down the Red Deer River—"the crookedest of all rivers"—to Grand Forks, Dakota. The steamboat was loaded with steel rails for the Canadian Pacific Railway which was then being built. Settlers were pouring in from all over the world and new places were springing up in all directions. In the Winnipeg district, in Texas, and at the other outposts of the Agency during that period, one of the most difficult tasks was to report the mushroom cities that continually sprang up "at the end of the track," as the new railways advanced across the prairies. Each of these had a very considerable percentage of traders who sought credit, opened their stores — sometimes quite pretentious ones —and then suddenly disappeared, leaving a few empty boxes and barrels and a multitude of unpaid bills behind them.

Washington, D. C., Office
Established 1890
National Metropolitan Bank Building

The opening of the office at Melbourne, Australia, in 1887 merits a brief reference, as this was the first branch of the Agency to be established outside of North America and Europe. The office was opened by the manager at London, England, who made a special trip to Australia for the purpose. Resident agents were appointed at the business centers of Western Australia, South Australia, New South Wales, Queensland and New Zealand. All of these districts are now covered by separate offices.

During the two decades the history of which has been briefly chronicled in this chapter the number of offices in The Mercantile Agency's chain increased from 28 to 126, a gain of exactly 350 per cent. In the United States and Canada the Agency's service was extended into practically every region then inhabited, while abroad the service was greatly strengthened by the new offices in Europe and the outpost in Australia. By 1890 the domestic field had been so thoroughly covered that the need of additional offices was only felt occasionally in districts where the population and volume of mercantile transactions were increasing with the greatest rapidity. It was to the foreign field that The Mercantile Agency now had to turn to find the greatest opportunities for expansion and the further enlargement of its usefulness.

CHAPTER VI

The Agency Expands Into a World-Wide Organization

1891–1916

DURING the first half century of its existence the growth of The Mercantile Agency was confined largely to the United States and Canada, only five of its 126 offices having been established elsewhere—four in Europe and one in Australia. During the last quarter of a century, and particularly during the last fifteen years, the history of the Agency has been a record of expansion in Europe, Africa, Australasia and Latin America that has placed it in the first rank among international organizations and carried the system inaugurated by Lewis Tappan into every corner of the globe. Out of the total of 115 new offices established during this period no less than 83 were located outside of the United States, and of these 77 were opened since 1900.

In 1891 and 1892 six new offices were established, as follows: Vancouver and Winston-Salem in 1891; and Trenton, Quebec, Ottawa and Wilkes-Barre in 1892. In 1893 new offices were opened at Zanesville, Ohio, and Charleston, W. Va. In February of the same year the list of Mr. Dun's partners was reduced to two—Arthur J. King and Robert Dun

Douglass. Six months later Mr. Dun established, under the management and personal supervision of Mr. Douglass, DUN'S REVIEW, a journal of finance and trade that has since been published every Saturday, and is generally recognized as the national authority on business conditions. The first number was issued August 5th, 1893, and the periodical at once became the medium for the publication of the failure returns sent in by all offices in the United States and Canada. Another feature, which was likewise an outgrowth of the trade circulars that had been published by the firm for many years, was the weekly summary of business conditions, based upon reports received from all the Agency managers throughout the United States and Canada. The REVIEW at present also publishes a weekly and monthly compilation of bank exchanges, a monthly record of building permits, and an Index Number and other statistics as to the prices of commodities. From time to time it issues special reports regarding the crop situation throughout the country that are widely copied, and the first of each year prepares a valuable general review of the business situation in the United States and Canada.

In February, 1894, the first Mercantile Agency Manual was published. This was a compilation of rulings on various questions and special information for the benefit of managers that was prepared at the express request of Mr. Dun. The first edition comprised regulations and instructions that had been issued in special circulars to the managers from time to time since **1883**. In later editions the valuable material contained in this publication has been kept

ROBERT DUN DOUGLASS
Associated with the management of The Mercantile Agency for
forty-four years, and present head of Board of Trustees

constantly revised and up to date, and the size of the book has steadily expanded until at present it com-

141

prises 190 pages, the general index consisting of near-ly 450 items. In 1897 a separate Reporters' Manual was issued, a publication that has since been reissued at occasional intervals.

In 1894, no doubt in consequence of the panic of the year before, no new branch offices were established. In 1895 only one was opened—at Canton, Ohio—and in 1896 no additions were made to the Agency's chain. On September 28th of that year Arthur J. King died at his residence, Bloomfield, N. J., after forty-seven years of service in The Mercantile Agency. Mr. King was born near London, England, in 1824, and came to this country when a young man, entering the New York office of the Agency as a clerk. He was the first manager of the office at Cleveland, then became manager at Cincinnati, and was afterward manager for eleven years at St. Louis. He was called to New York in 1880, and was a partner in the business and the general manager at the time of his death. He was a man of high character, inflexible in his devotion to principle, and of unusual business ability. Mr. King was succeeded as general manager by Robert Dun Douglass, who was Mr. Dun's only partner for the remainder of the latter's lifetime.

In December, 1897, an office was opened at Mexico City—the first branch of the Agency in Latin America. Mexico was then enjoying the benefits of the longest period of peace and prosperity in the history of the republic. American and European capital was being invested in all parts of the country and its vast

natural resources were beginning to be developed.
Railroads were in course of construction in regions
where they were most needed, and costly port works
were inaugurated by the government in order to afford safe harbors for the ships that this internal activity brought in increasing numbers. The time was
seen to be most auspi-
cious for the estab-
lishment of an office to
report to exporters
in Europe a n d the
United States regard-
ing the standing and
antecedents of the
firms that were then
seeking credit abroad.
Some of these were
new American or
European houses es-
tablished as a result
of the influx of for-
eign capital, others
were concerns that

Mexico City Office
Established 1897
2a Capuchinas No. 48

had existed for years, but were now doing a larger
business. There were new electric light and power
companies, new mines and plantations, new factories
in several lines, new trading houses in every State.
In 1901 the volume of business necessitated opening a suboffice at Guadalajara. Others were established from year to year, until by 1907 there were

143

seven offices of The Mercantile Agency in Mexico. The Agency's system in Mexico was at that date so complete that practically every business concern of any importance in the republic was reported, its list of correspondents covering every state, and nearly every town. These records have been saved and will prove of inestimable value when business conditions become normal again, not only to merchants in the United States and Europe granting credits in Mexico to houses known to be responsible, but to all such houses as well. During the recent troubles the suboffices have been kept open as far as possible, and the head office at Mexico City has never closed. The annals of The Mercantile Agency contain no finer example of courage and devotion than that displayed by its staff in Mexico since the retirement of Porfirio Diaz.

On November 17th, 1897, announcement was made in Boston and vicinity of an important change in the Boston office of The Mercantile Agency and the four suboffices in that district, as follows:

> The undersigned, sole proprietor of The Mercantile Agency, who has conducted its business since 1851, under style of Edward Russell & Co., with partners, successively, George William Gordon, Edwin F. Waters, George A. Priest, and George H. Hull, Jr., none of them now living, admonished by advancing years of his necessary retirement ere long, and desiring repose after fifty-three years' continuous service in the Agency, avails himself of the friendly offer of Messrs. R. G. Dun & Co. to assume the business of his offices in Boston, Worcester, Lynn, Portland and Bangor from January 1st, 1898.   Edward Russell.

144

FRANCIS L. MINTON AND BENJAMIN DOUGLASS, JR.

Two advisers who have aided in shaping the executive policies of R. G. DUN & CO., The Mercantile Agency, for more than forty years

In actual operation, the relations between Edward Russell & Co. and **R. G. Dun & Co.,** and the latter's various predecessors, were always so intimate that, in so far as the interests of subscribers were concerned, the two were virtually a single concern. Mr. Russell during his long career constantly maintained the highest standards of The Mercantile Agency, and always cordially co-operated with the management at New York in promptly extending to his part of the system every improvement that was made in theirs. He retired from the business enjoying in the highest degree the esteem of his former associates and the respect and good-will of the mercantile community throughout New England.

The year 1898 was a memorable one, because it witnessed the completion of the beautiful Dun Building at the northeast corner of Reade Street and Broadway, now familiar wherever The Mercantile Agency is known as the home of the head office at New York. From 1841 to 1845 the address of The Mercantile Agency (then Lewis Tappan & Co.) was Hanover Street, corner of Exchange Place. From 1846 to 1849 the address was 9 Exchange Place, and from 1850 to 1853 it was 70 Cedar Street. From 1854 to 1857 the address was 111 Broadway, and from then until 1860 was given as 111 Broadway and 314 Broadway. It then became 314 Broadway only, and in fact that number is alone given in the Reference Books of 1859 and 1860. The office remained at that number during the war, but from 1865 to 1867 it was

A portion of the eleventh floor of the Dun Building

This handsome room is finished in white Italian marble throughout. The executive offices of The Mercantile Agency are now all located on this floor

147

located at 293-295 Broadway—or directly opposite the present building, which is No. 290. From 1868 to January, 1878, the address was 335 Broadway, but between January and July, 1878, the office was moved back to its old location 314-316 Broadway, where it remained until the new building was completed twenty years later.

It was originally planned to erect a building twenty-one stories in height, but Mr. Dun felt that there were enough "sky-scrapers," as structures over twenty stories high were then called, and the edifice as finally completed had only fifteen floors. As it now stands the edifice is 223 feet in height from the sidewalk to the sill of the roof, the flagstaff rising 70 feet higher, while the basement and sub-basement extend 30 feet below the street level. Architecturally it is regarded as one of the most graceful and beautiful office structures in America. The exterior is granite, faced with white marble, while the entrance hall and the grand staircase on the ground floor are in Sienna marble from Italy. All of the wood used in the structure is fireproof, having been treated by an electric process used by many navies in the interior construction of warships. Many remarkable tests of wood thus treated were made at the time, and in March, 1900, a fire actually broke out in the building which destroyed all the furniture in one room. The blaze was so fierce that iron hinges were twisted and glass melted, but the woodwork was merely scorched and the fire easily confined to the room in which it

The thirteenth floor of the Dun Building showing some of the cases containing records for the West, and a portion of the small army of typists, pasters and other clerks employed in the Department of the South and West started. The building is equipped with its own electric light and power plant, steam being supplied by two 300-h.p. boilers, while the generating sets are located under the Broadway sidewalk. To improve the economy and regulation of these generators, and to enable the light and power to be supplied from one generator without too great a fluctuation in the voltage, a storage battery of 114 cells of chloride accumulators has been installed on the roof. In addition to supplying current for the electric lights in the building this plant furnishes the power for six Sprague screw-type electric elevators, an ash hoist, a sidewalk elevator and a 72-inch fan—all motor driven—together with a pump to supply water to all floors. The building also contains a 10-ton refrigerating plant for furnishing ice water to the tenants and for the use of a restaurant that is located in the basement.

As the building was erected primarily as the head office of The Mercantile Agency, the six upper floors, from the tenth to the fifteenth, were expressly designed to meet the needs of the business. In recent years the whole of the ninth floor has also been occupied by the firm for its own offices and about May 1st of the present year (1916), the first floor was taken also. The executive offices are on the eleventh floor and are handsomely finished in Pavonoza marble. Some years ago a business magazine published a picture of the eleventh floor in a series of illustrations entitled "Famous Battlefields of Business." The

The first floor of the Dun Building, showing a general view of the City Department, including the new mezzanine gallery erected to accommodate a portion of the many clerks here employed. This department also occupies portions of three other floors

railed-off section occupied by the general manager and his assistants might better be likened to the headquarters of the general staff of a great army, for around the broad mahogany table at which the manager sits matters are decided that affect every office in the Agency's world-wide chain, and influence the activities of each of its many thousands of employees.

The City Department occupies all of the first floor, with its mezzanine gallery, half of the second, part of the seventh, and most of the fifteenth floors. In this department are recorded the reports covering the enormous commercial activities of the City of New York in all of its five boroughs. The twelfth floor is occupied by the Eastern Department, and the thirteenth and fourteenth by the Department of the South and West, the latter also including Canada. The tenth floor is occupied by the Collection Department, while the ninth contains the Foreign Department, the Reference Book Department and the offices of DUN'S REVIEW.

Another interesting event in the year 1898 was the establishment of The Mercantile Agency Mutual Benefit Association by a number of the employees of the New York office, for the purpose of providing a fund from which death benefits could be paid. All the employees, without exception, were declared eligible, irrespective of age, physical condition, or any of the considerations that usually apply in undertakings of this character. Under the plan adopted, the payment of five cents per week provides for a death benefit of $200, while for ten cents a week, the amount of the benefit has been fixed at $300.

During the eighteen years of the Association's existence, benefits to the number of 121 have been paid, or a total of $28,500. The Association had to its credit January 1st, 1916, funds, securely invested or deposited in savings banks, amounting to $15,-889.85. While the creation of this surplus was partly due to contributions by the firm, the Association, notwithstanding the liberal terms under which its benefits are provided, has been able to meet all its obligations from the annual dues, interest on investments, and the proceeds of annual entertainments, which all connected with the business, from owners to route boys, look forward to, attend, and heartily enjoy.

In 1898 one branch office was established—at Menominee, Mich., its district including the rich copper and iron fields in the Upper Peninsula of Michigan and the vast lumber region of northwestern Wisconsin. In 1899 an office was established at Havana, Cuba. It proved successful from the very start and has been most helpful to the mercantile interests of the Island as well as to European and American merchants extending credit there.

During the year 1900, by a somewhat remarkable coincidence, the two men who had been successively at the head of The Mercantile Agency for more than fifty years passed away within a few months of one another. On May 4th, Benjamin Douglass, the second proprietor of the Agency, died at Santa Bar-

bara, Cal. On disposing of his interest in the institution to Mr. Dun in 1859, Mr. Douglass virtually retired from business, but in 1876 he again entered the service of The Mercantile Agency as manager of the Chicago office and district. This position he retained until January 1st, 1889, eleven years before his death. This was a period of thirteen years, and—curiously enough—it was for an equal period that he was previously connected with the Agency, from 1846 to 1859. One is strongly reminded of the famous example of John Quincy Adams who, after having been President of the United States, became a member of Congress from Massachusetts, and for many years served his State and the nation with distinguished success in this humbler capacity without in any way lessening his dignity or fame. In the same way Mr. Douglass after having played a conspicuous part as one of the founders and early proprietors of The Mercantile Agency, achieved a new success and won the respect and esteem of all who came in contact with him in his later position of district manager. In addition to his remarkable business ability, Mr. Douglass was a fine Hebrew and Greek scholar and a writer of great force and clearness. His handwriting, many examples of which are still preserved in the archives of the Agency, resembled engraving in its neatness and legibility.

On November 10th, 1900—or slightly more than six months after the death of his former partner—Robert Graham Dun, the sole proprietor of The Mercantile Agency, died at his New York residence. He had been associated with the Agency for nearly half a century and its sole owner since 1859. He had been intimately associated with its growth from a loosely united group of seven small offices, having less than 75 employees, to a powerful institution of world-wide renown, with 140 offices and several thousand employees. At the time of his death many hundreds of newspapers noted the event and published sketches of his career. One of the best summaries, however, of the qualities that in a great measure account for his success, appeared in the *National Cyclopedia of American Biography,* published in 1899:

> In New York, where he is well known, Mr. Dun is universally respected for his high integrity, broad and liberal views, exceeding amiability, good judgment, and his love of art. His special attribute, however, has been his insight into character, and his ability to secure and retain the services of men of a high degree of capacity and energy, so that he has constantly augmented the army of capable and reliable people about him. The men of high ability whom this Agency employs in every city, and the excellent local standing of its representatives everywhere, are evidences of this. Few names are more prominent in commercial circles than that of Robert Graham Dun, while as the head of a great instrumentality of commerce in especial relation to the granting of credits, Mr. Dun has attracted the attention of the people at large.

Emerson has said that "an institution is the lengthening shadow of one man." Partly by reason of his great gift in choosing his associates, The Mercantile Agency that bears the name of R. G. DUN & Co. is the "lengthening shadow" of many men. It bears indelibly impressed upon its organization the marks of Lewis Tappan, its founder. Many of its most fundamental characteristics are due to Benjamin Douglass, who had charge of its destinies during the formative period when its principles and policies were determined for all time. Some of the most important features of the Agency service of to-day were planned and inaugurated under the direct personal supervision of one or another of Mr. Dun's associates in the executive management of the business, or were the result of the joint efforts of the entire executive body. Countless improvements, many of them of great value, were suggested by branch office managers. No greater tribute can be paid to the memory of Mr. Dun than to recall the fact that during the forty-one years of his supreme control The Mercantile Agency continued to expand and to improve without interruption. There was no backward step. As men of old built monuments and temples to their memory, so Mr. Dun erected during these forty-one years a monument more durable than bronze or stone—the great institution that bears his name.

Since Mr. Dun's death the business has been conducted under a trusteeship, the trustees after the death of Mrs. Dun being Robert Dun Douglass, Francis L. Minton and Thomas James. Mr. James had previously been connected with the work of the Agency for a number of years and on his death, in 1912, was succeeded as trustee by Joseph Packard.

In 1901 the executive management at New York inaugurated a policy of world-wide expansion that has made the last fifteen years as notable as any period in the history of the Agency. Up to that time the branches at London, Paris, Berlin, etc., were not reporting offices like those in the United States and Canada, but confined their work to collecting credit information regarding such firms in their respective districts as had been or were likely to be inquired about in this country.

Every foreign office was now instructed to collect reports regarding all of the principal traders in its district, and to offer the information thus secured to local clients as well as to those abroad. This broader sphere of action resulted in a vast increase in the volume of business transacted and necessitated the rapid establishment of suboffices in every district. Simultaneously with this expansion in the regions already covered by the Agency's service, the executives at New York took vigorous steps to establish the organization in countries that it had never hitherto reached. There is no "romance of business" more fascinating than the record of these fifteen years. It is a record of achievement in widely scattered fields, and under profoundly dissimilar conditions, that, taken as a whole, has few parallels in the annals of American business expansion in foreign lands.

The very first office established after the new policy had been decided upon affords an excellent example of its results and a striking illustration of its wisdom.

This was the branch at Cape Town, South Africa, which was opened in 1901. The Boer War, which began in October, 1899, was then still in progress. The annexation of the Transvaal had been proclaimed September 1st, 1900, and that of the Orange Free State May 24th of the same year, but hostilities did not cease until May 31st, 1902. There were many who considered this a peculiarly inopportune time to inaugurate the business of The Mercantile Agency in that country. Mr. Douglass, on the other hand, insisted that it was the psychological moment to launch such an enterprise. The result vindicated his judgment and foresight in a remarkable manner.

By entering the field at this time it was possible to secure reports regarding practically all the important concerns that had been engaged in business in South Africa before the war, as well as to keep track of the numerous changes that took place during the years of the conflict. Thus equipped, the Agency, by the time peace was restored and business conditions began to return to their normal state, possessed a mass of data that no later comer in the territory could ever hope to duplicate. It thus came to be recognized both in South Africa and in Europe as the foremost authority on all matters relating to the financial standing of South African traders, and particularly regarding the credit record of houses that were in existence before the war, or the partners in such houses who afterward undertook new enterprises. The growth in the volume of South African business was so rapid that in 1903—the year after the close of hostilities—a suboffice was opened at Johannesburg. This was followed by another suboffice at Port Elizabeth in 1904, and one at Durban in 1905, making a chain of four South African offices established in four years.

Some conception of the courage required to establish these offices may be obtained from the fact that a very large amount was expended in South Africa before the business there became self-supporting. This is the invariable experience in opening new offices in a virgin field, since large sums are required to collect and record the data regarding the many thousands or tens of thousands of business houses in such districts before clients can be called upon to pay one penny for reports. Subscribers to foreign reports frequently overlook this fact. The collection of information in South Africa during war time was especially difficult and costly, but the effort was more than justified by the fact, as already noted, that much of the data thus secured could never have been obtained afterward.

The establishment of a branch office of the Agency at Berlin, Germany, has already been mentioned. The new policy with respect to the foreign offices involved a change in the service rendered that proved to be exceptionally well adapted to the needs of the business community in the German Empire. Not only were commerce and industry in that country highly developed, so that the value of this new facility for the further safeguarding of credits was instantly appreciated, but the vast extent of Germany's foreign trade, both export and import, rendered the overseas service of The Mercantile Agency especially helpful. The result was an expansion of the business in Germany that necessitated the opening of one suboffice after another in rapid succession until the Agency's chain in the German Empire alone numbered twenty-three offices, in addition to which five branches were established in Austria-Hungary and three in the Netherlands that were subsidiary to the head office in Germany. Of these no less than four were opened in 1901, beginning with the office at Hamburg, which was established in February of that year. Following is a list of the offices of The Mercantile Agency in Germany, Austria-Hungary and the Netherlands, with the dates on which they were established:

Berlin	1876	Munich	1906
Hamburg	1901	Budapest	1907
Bremen	1901	Prague	1907
Cologne	1901	Dresden	1907
Frankfort a/M.	1901	Dusseldorf	1907
Leipzig	1902	Plauen	1907
Breslau	1902	Stuttgart	1907
Magdeburg	1902	Elberfeld	1908
Amsterdam	1902	Trieste	1908
Vienna	1904	Strassburg	1908
Rotterdam	1905	Konigsberg	1912
Mannheim	1906	Saarbrucken	1912
Hanover	1906	Erfurt	1912
Nuremberg	1906	Lemberg	1914
Danzig	1906	The Hague	1914
Dortmund	1906		

The year 1901 also witnessed a further expansion of the Agency's service in Australia, an office being

Johannesburg Office (1903)
National Mutual Buildings

Cape Town Office (1901)
Mansion House Chambers

The Mercantile Agency now has four offices in South Africa

Durban Office (1905)
Natal Bank Chambers

established during that year at Sydney, New South Wales. The Melbourne office had been in operation since 1887, but was largely used for the purpose of securing information regarding Australian traders for the benefit of shippers in other parts of the world. Under the new policy just inaugurated, the activities of the Australian district began to include reporting both Australian and foreign houses for the benefit of Australian merchants and manufacturers. This necessitated there, as elsewhere, a rapid expansion of the facilities for collecting and recording the necessary information. Instead of only carrying on their records reports concerning houses engaged in foreign trade, the Agency in Australia now sought to report all traders just as was done in the United States and Canada. The new branch at Sydney was made the head office for the Commonwealth, which was proclaimed on January 1st of the very year of its establishment. The subsequent expansion of the business of The Mercantile Agency in Australasia was rapid. In 1902, a suboffice was established at Brisbane, the capital of Queensland. In 1903 suboffices were opened at Adelaide, South Australia, and at Wellington, New Zealand—that Dominion also forming a part of the Sydney district. In 1908 three additional offices were opened in New Zealand—at Auckland, Christchurch and Dunedin—and in 1913 the Agency's chain of offices in the state capitals of Australia was made com-

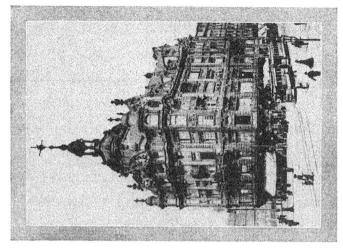

Dresden Office (1907)
Pragerstrasse 54

Berlin Office (1876)
Corner Friedrichstrasse and Kochstrasse

Rotterdam Office (1905)
Coolsingel 22

The Mercantile Agency has at present 31 offices in Germany, Austria-Hungary and the Netherlands

plete by the establishment of a branch at Perth, Western Australia.

The Paris office, like those at London and Berlin, was greatly strengthened by the new policy enabling it to do a local as well as an international business. It was not until 1902 that this plan was extended to the Paris district. The effect was immediate. In thirty years the staff had only increased from three employees, the number in 1872, to five. The very year of the change in policy the first suboffice was opened at Brussels, Belgium—and by the following year the staff at Paris had increased to twenty. The Paris district comprised all of Western Europe, including France, Belgium, Switzerland, Italy, Spain and Portugal, together with Egypt, Tunis and Algeria. Altogether, the Paris staff has to translate reports in no less than twelve languages. The energy with which the district was developed is indicated by the fact that in 1903 suboffices were established at

Sydney, N. S. W., Office
Established 1901
Challis House, Martin Place

Melbourne Office (1887)
60 Queen Street

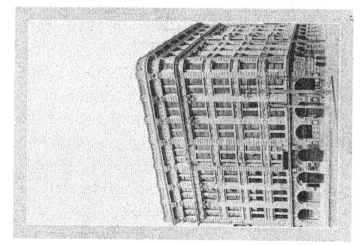

Wellington Office (1903)
Nathan's Building

The Mercantile Agency has nine offices in Australia and New Zealand

Brisbane Office (1902)
334, 336 and 338 Queen Street

Barcelona, Spain; Havre and Lille, France; Zurich, Switzerland, and Milan, Italy. The complete list of offices opened in these countries with their respective dates, is as follows:

FRANCE

Havre	1903
Lille	1903
Paris	1872

BELGIUM

Antwerp	1904
Brussels	1902
Liege	1912

SWITZERLAND

Zurich	1903

PORTUGAL

Lisbon	1906
Oporto	1912

SPAIN

Barcelona	1903
Bilbao	1912
Madrid	1906
Malaga	1912
Murcia	1912
Seville	1913
Valencia	1912

ITALY

Milan	1903
Naples	1912
Turin	1915

The year 1902, which marks the beginning of the period of active development and expansion in the business of The Mercantile Agency in Western Europe, is also memorable as the date when the first extension of its service was made to South America. The pioneer office on that continent was located at Buenos Aires, its district including not only Argentina but the republics of Paraguay and Uruguay. A suboffice was established at Rosario in 1913. In 1912, in response to the urgent requests of business men in that country, an independent branch office was opened at Rio de Janeiro, Brazil. The chain of offices in Latin America, which comprises in addition to the three just mentioned seven in Mexico and one in Cuba, has recently been supplemented by the establishment of a branch at San Juan, Porto Rico. The other islands in the Caribbean region—Spanish, English, French, Danish and Dutch—are covered by an army of correspondents located in every trading center. These report direct to New York, as steamship communica-

The Paris Office, which was established in 1872, and is now located at 5 Boulevard Montmartre, is the head office for France, Belgium, Switzerland, Italy, Spain and Portugal

tions between that port and the various ports of the West Indies are more regular and frequent than those between many of the islands themselves.

The rapid expansion of the foreign service of The Mercantile Agency in 1901, 1902 and 1903—no less than 27 offices being opened abroad during those three years—suggested to the management the desirability

Bilbao Office, established in 1912, and located at Calle Estacion 5,
"Edificio Aurora"

of publishing an International Edition of Dun's Review in order to link this world-wide chain of offices
together through a publication in which all would be
equally interested. Accordingly, in March, 1903, the
first number of Dun's International Review was
issued. The publication met with immediate success,

Milan Office, established in 1903, and located at Via Orefici 1,
(Piazza del Duomo)

168

and a few months later a separate edition in Spanish was inaugurated. It has since been published in two monthly editions, English and Spanish, and is recognized as a leader in the field of international journalism. Its advertising clients comprise several hundred of the leading manufacturers seeking foreign markets, and it is interesting to note that its patronage has been drawn from sixteen different countries and has included four Governments. In this respect it is more truly an international paper than any publication in its field. A feature of the International Edition of DUN's REVIEW of great value to business men every-

Buenos Aires Office
Established 1902
Banco Germanico Building

where is its series of reports on trade conditions, prepared by the managers of the foreign offices of The Mercantile Agency or by the REVIEW's own correspondents in countries where offices have not yet been established.

169

Another branch of the organization that is directly due to the Agency's offices abroad is the Foreign Department. Here are kept constantly on file the reports regarding many thousands of concerns in every part of the world. Whenever a report on any foreign firm is requested in the United States or Canada it is procured, if not already on file, and branch offices abroad also send to New York all reports that are likely to be inquired for there. In addition to these, copies of all reports written up regarding firms in South America, Central America and the West Indies are filed at New York. This means that a manufacturer doing business abroad—and especially in Latin America and the West Indies—can, in many cases, secure a report regarding a prospective customer without waiting for the information to come from the country in question, the data he needs to determine his prospect's credit responsibility being already recorded at New York. This is an inestimable benefit to exporters, since a delay in the foreign trade frequently means loss of orders.

Havana Office
Established 1899
Banco Nacional de Cuba Building

It should not be concluded from the amount of space devoted in this chapter to the extension of The Mercantile Agency in other lands that its growth in the United States and Canada was arrested during this period. On the contrary, the last fifteen years have brought a steady series of additions to the Agency chain. Naturally, however, most of the new offices are in places of somewhat less importance than those previously established, owing to the thoroughness with which the new offices opened in the seventies and eighties covered the more important points in every district. The list on page 172 shows the new offices in the United States and Canada established between 1891 and

Rio de Janeiro Office
Established 1912
Jornal do Brasil Building

July, 1916, with the date of each. Of these ten were in Canada, all of them located in the Canadian Northwest. The principal development in the United States was in the South, Southwest and West.

Vancouver	1891	Muskogee	1909
Winston-Salem	1891	Pensacola	1909
Trenton	1892	Greenville	1910
Quebec	1892	Edmonton	1910
Ottawa	1892	Butte	1910
Wilkes-Barre	1892	Regina	1910
Zanesville	1893	Saskatoon	1910
Charleston, W. Va.	1893	Easton	1910
Canton, O.	1895	Victoria, B. C.	1910
Menominee	1898	Beaver Falls	1911
Oklahoma	1902	Abilene	1911
Youngstown	1902	Amarillo	1911
Beaumont	1902	San Diego	1911
Meridian	1902	Moose Jaw	1912
Selma	1902	Lethbridge	1913
Columbia, S. C.	1902	Jamestown	1914
Green Bay	1903	Oakland	1914
Albuquerque	1903	Sacramento	1914
Tampa	1905	Phœnix	1914
Waterloo	1905	Paterson	1914
Calgary	1906	Tulsa	1916
Harrisburg	1908	Terre Haute	1916

*New Mezzanine Gallery on first floor of the Dun Building
Where the dictaphone operators of the City Department are
located. Dictaphones are largely used in this Department*

As early as 1860 a printing department was established to take care of the Reference Book and the numerous forms used in the business. This plant was first located at 10-12 Reade Street. In May, 1871, it was removed to 83 Centre Street, where it was totally destroyed by fire on Christmas eve, 1872. The next location was at 148 Worth Street, and in 1882 a large printing house was erected at 57-59 Park Street. Here an entire floor was occupied by the presses on which the Reference Books were printed, the second floor was arranged for the compositors and proofreaders, while the third contained the job department where blanks and other stationery were printed. The bindery occupied the remainder of the third floor

Charleston, W. Va., Office
Established 1893
Citizens' National Bank Building

and the whole of the fourth and fifth. The cases on the second floor in this building contained more than seventy-five tons of agate type alone, and the entire plant was valued at upward of $250,000.

The growth of the business, however, made even this plant inadequate, and an additional building was erected for the presses on which the INTERNATIONAL

173

REVIEW was printed as early as 1905. The increase in the size of the Reference Book and in the number of copies required presently made the entire establishment overcrowded, especially at the seasons when the work on the January and July books was going on. In 1913 the City of New York acquired the site occupied by the Park Street plant for the proposed civic center in connection with the new Court House, and the firm then began the erection of a new and much larger printing house at the northwest corner of Butler and N e v i n s Streets, in the Borough of Brooklyn.

Butte, Mont., Office
Established 1910
First National Bank Building

This establishment, which was completed and occupied on August 1st, 1914, is regarded as one of the most up-to-date printing offices in the United States. The building is of reinforced concrete, 200 feet long by 100 feet wide, and is four stories in height. On the ground floor are located the office of the Superintendent, the pressroom and the shipping and stock rooms. The pressroom contains eight flat-bed presses and two Cottrell rotary presses of the latest type, capable of printing on both sides, folding and delivering eighty-five 32-page forms of the Reference Book per minute. There are also five

174

job platen presses for short runs and miscellaneous job work. On the second floor are 10 linotype machines, the entire Reference Book now being set on these machines instead of by hand composition as before. Adjacent to the machines are the cabinets where the 3,174 page forms of the book are kept in n u m b e r e d racks, r e a d y to be taken out at any time for corrections, a n d then sent to the stereo-type room, which is on the same floor, where plates are made for the pressroom. The third floor contains the bindery, w h i c h has been m o d e r n i z e d throughout to corre-spond with the other branches of the new plant, and is now able to bind close to 1,000 copies of the Refer-

Old Printing House of R. G. DUN & CO.
at 57-59 Park Street
Occupied from 1882 to 1911

ence Book per day. In addition to printing and binding the Reference Book, the printing house prints and binds the weekly and monthly editions of DUN's REVIEW and the pocket editions of the Reference Book, besides turning out stationery and forms for the vari-

175

ous offices throughout the country. Motor cars carry work between this department and the head office, and deliver Reference Books throughout the city.

With the opening of the office at Terre Haute, Ind., in July, 1916, the number of offices in The Mercantile Agency amounted to 243, besides 24 reporting stations, some of which are as large as offices. The

New Printing House of R. G. DUN & CO.
Corner of Butler and Nevins Streets, in the Borough of Brooklyn.
Reinforced concrete, four stories high, 200 feet long and 100 feet wide

epoch-making changes produced by the world war will necessitate new extensions in the foreign field, while the process of ceaseless growth in the United States and Canada will bring about gradual additions to the Agency's chain of offices in this country and in the Dominion. Considered in its broadest sense, the function of The Mercantile Agency is to keep abreast of the progress of mankind in all matters relating to credit. As the pioneers of civilization have pushed

Portion of the pressroom, showing flat-bed presses used for printing the weekly and monthly editions of DUN'S REVIEW

farther into the undeveloped regions of the world the Agency has followed them, for capital as well as labor

The two Cottrell rotary presses for printing the Reference Book. Each machine prints, folds and delivers 2,720 pages per minute

is needed in all such enterprises, and capital can never be forthcoming unless the credit qualifications of those who seek it have first been carefully determined.

177

When The Mercantile Agency was established at New York by Lewis Tappan in 1841 it was the first institution of its kind in the world. Under Benjamin Douglass it was strengthened as to its policies and methods and made national in scope. Under Robert Graham Dun it was expanded until it covered the United States and Canada with a network of offices,

The composing room in the Printing House, showing battery of linotype machines (at left) and part of the cabinets in which the page forms of the Reference Book are kept

while the volume of its transactions far exceeded the wildest visions of its founders. Under Robert Dun Douglass it has been once more expanded into a world-wide organization, and the magnitude of its transactions again multiplied.

Robert Dun Douglass first entered the service of the Agency in 1872 and has been intimately associated with its management ever since—a period of forty-four years. Most of those connected with the great institution to-day have known no other chief, and in them all he has inspired an intense spirit of loyalty to the Agency and of personal devotion to himself. On January 1st, 1910, Mr. Douglass decided to relinquish the cares and responsibilities of general manager, but as one of the Trustees he continues to direct the policies of the business and to promote its further expansion and prosperity.

Closely associated with Mr. Douglass in the direction of the Agency in recent years have been his fellow Trustees, Francis L. Minton and Joseph Packard. Mr. Minton has been connected with the institution, as an adviser and director, for more than forty years. and has been a member of the Board of Trustees since the death of Mr. Dun. His tireless energy, extensive legal knowledge and sound judgment have contributed materially to the progress of the organization throughout the period covered by this chapter. Another pilot of the business for over forty years is Benjamin Douglass, Jr., whose judicious judgment has often been of inestimable service to the executives of the institution, and whose vision has never been clouded by any ill-temper nor distorted by any unworthy purpose. The present General Manager of The Mercantile Agency is A. W. Ferguson, who has occupied that position since 1910. In a record covering nearly three generations it is impossible to mention individually the hundreds of managers and heads of departments whose work, in their respective fields, has contributed so much to the success of the organization. In a way this entire history is a tribute to them, since—but for their efficiency in their respective tasks, their loyalty and devotion to the organization as a whole—this record of 75 years of continuous progress would never have been written.

Almost from its very inception, the words "For the Promotion and Protection of Trade" have been the motto of The Mercantile Agency. For seventy-five years every effort of the institution has been directed to fulfilling the mission expressed by that motto. As it has grown greater, as its operations have been extended into broader fields, as its activities have become more complex, it has been enabled to fulfill that mission to a higher degree. To-day its methods represent the accumulated experience, and its vast collections of reports the accumulated information of three-quarters of a century. As its annals show, the process of improvement has been continuous during all these years, yet the cost of the Agency's service to its subscribers is actually less than it was in 1841.

In an Agency circular published thirty-five years ago appears the following passage:

> The advance made in business facilities is greater than the improvement attained in any other department of human activity. The telegraph, the telephone, railroads; cheap, frequent and rapid posts; banking, insurance, expressage, exchanges and associations with limited liability—are all agencies so common in every day's experience that one hardly realizes how recent is the in-

troduction of most of them into ordinary use. Yet, notwithstanding the perfection in the growth of all business facilities, uncertainties attend every business man's career, and none are more disastrous than the losses incurred by the injudicious granting of credits. The first organized effort ever made to lessen the chances of loss in this direction is The Mercantile Agency.

While its object has remained unchanged, the facilities for attaining that object have enlarged far beyond the dreams of its founders. As the foregoing pages show, the growth of the institution has kept pace with the growth of the nation, and in the last twenty-five years its expansion has been world-wide in response to the vast increase in international commerce and the rapid development of far-off regions like Australia and South Africa.

Modern commerce is based upon credit to an extent scarcely realized by those who have not given the subject special attention. Credit is founded upon confidence, and confidence, in turn, is derived from accurate and impartial information. The commercial world now realizes more than ever before the extent of its reliance upon such a service as The Mercantile Agency was expressly designed to supply, and to the improvement of which it has devoted seventy-five years of continuous effort and accumulated experience. It is hoped that this outline of the annals of the Agency will enable those who are associated with it to realize more fully the greatness of the institution of which they form a part, and increase their pride in it and in their work. It is also hoped that the book

181

may assist those who are engaged in the granting of credits to a better understanding of the history of The Mercantile Agency, and that students of economic and of business methods will find it valuable as the record of an institution that was the first of its kind, and that has been, throughout its long history, a pioneer in bringing about sound credit conditions for the promotion and protection of trade throughout the world.

CPSIA information can be obtained
at www.ICGtesting.com
Printed in the USA
BVHW04*1321090818
524035BV00006B/55/P